Lift High the Banner

All the very best!

Julie C. Marlow

And G—D said, Let there be light: and there was light. Gen. 1:3

LIFT HIGH THE BANNER

Secrets of a Sephardic Messianic Jewish Family Revealed

Julie C. Marlow

WESTBOW
PRESS
A DIVISION OF THOMAS NELSON

ISBN: 978-1-4497-0909-9 (sc)
ISBN: 978-1-4497-2406-1 (hc)
ISBN: 978-1-4497-2407-8 (e)

Library of Congress Control Number: 2011914714

WestBow Press books may be ordered through booksellers or by contacting:

WestBow Press
A Division of Thomas Nelson
1663 Liberty Drive
Bloomington, IN 47403
www.westbowpress.com
1-(866) 928-1240

Printed in the United States of America

WestBow Press rev. date: 04/26/2012

CONTENTS

DEDICATION

This book is dedicated to my wonderful Mother, Jennie Cordova, and to the loving memory of my Father, Joseph D. Cordova, for their love, encouragement and, especially, for their example of godly living that inspired all of us children to seek our own personal relationship with our Lord and Savior, Yeshua HaMashiach (Jesus the Messiah).

"The father of the righteous shall greatly rejoice: and he that begetteth a wise child shall have joy of him.

Thy father and thy mother shall be glad, and she that bare thee shall rejoice." (Proverbs 23: 24-25) KJV

ACKNOWLEDGEMENTS

First, my deepest gratitude goes to my Lord and Savior for giving me the dream of writing a non-fiction book about my family's religious history and legacy. Without the inspiration and help from Him, obtained from reading and studying the Family Bible, this book may never have been written.

I want to give a special thanks to my dear mother, Jennie Cordova, who helped me get started by going to the Allen County Public Library in Fort Wayne, Indiana, to research our family genealogy. It was not an easy job for her to sit at a microfilm machine for hours at a time. I am grateful for her love of family that encouraged me to step out with this project. She means so much to me.

My sincere gratitude to my dear husband, Arthur D. Marlow, for believing in me, for his patience, his words of encouragement and sound advice. I appreciate him standing beside me and giving generously of his time and support. He was an integral part of my vision and dream.

Also, I want to give my sincere appreciation to my daughter, Catherine (Marlow) Garrett, and my granddaughter, Meghan Elizabeth Garrett, for their contributions in editing this work. Their advice and helpful suggestions were greatly appreciated and their contributions made this book possible.

I would like to express special thanks to my assistant, Carole J. Branum, for her help in typing and modifying, as well as for her insight into my vision, which helped bring this book to life.

Additionally my thanks go to Teresa (Zutaut) Marlow, my daughter-in-law for her advice and helpful suggestions. I appreciate and thank my son,

Arthur Dixon Marlow, II, for his knowledge and technical support, my son-in-law, Jerry Michael Garrett, and my grandson, Ethan Michael Garrett. It was your help that kept me going.

My appreciation also to my brothers, Joseph Del, Richard and Daniel Cordova, for their help looking up information at libraries in states and countries that I could not personally visit.

To my helpful sisters, Marian Jordan, Sarah Yoder, Edna Hemsoth, Evelyn Archuleta. My friends, Guy Dean Benson, Vicki Butcher, Fran Henry, Inez and Leslie Lucas, a big thank you for your contributions of newspaper clippings, books, and other favors.

In addition, finally, my deepest appreciation to all those who prayed for this project and who will now see the results of their support.

INTRODUCTION

This book has been written from the heart, for the stories that my parents and grandparents shared with the older children in the family were told with great emotion. Some of my family members were reluctant to share secrets that had been kept for five hundred years. They remembered that their ancestors had wanted no written records kept, for fear their families would be discriminated against and persecuted.

My original purpose in writing this non-fiction book was to share only with my family, the results of the genealogical findings and research that I had been doing. Unlike me, the younger children in the family did not get to hear my parents and grandparents talk about their early lives. I want all of them to know what I learned from the oral history passed down from one generation to another, so that they can appreciate their rich heritage.

It was only recently that family members finally agreed with me that perhaps the time had come when God would allow them to safely reveal our history and our religious beliefs, including why our ancestors had felt it necessary to use coded surnames for many years.

This book is long overdue. After thinking about it for some time I decided this book should be shared with the public. I believe that anyone who reads this story will be amazed to learn that, even today, there are people living in this country who remember all too well the nightmare of being persecuted and discriminated against because of their loyalty to their ancient religious beliefs. I also realize that future generations of my family need to know this history. If it is not revealed now, the truth and the mysteries surrounding it could be lost forever.

Hopefully, my book will not offend nor hurt anyone feelings. History is what it is and should not be changed. As you read my book, I hope you will appreciate the source of my family's concerns.

The idea of this book began in 1970's, when God placed a desire in my heart to get serious about researching my family history and writing about it. Little did I know where this would lead me. What I discovered was far more than my parents or grandparents had told us. I am sure they were afraid to say too much, but they tried to share with the older children the history as far back as they could remember. It soon became apparent that many facts could not be recalled and the events of some years were completely missing. That made the history difficult to piece together.

My overall research encompassed a period that began in Old Testament days and ended 500 years later in approximately 2010. While I may not have included all pertinent historical facts for all those years, the history is as complete as possible in the way that I describe the beliefs, language and other interesting facts that I learned about my ancestors and the places where God scattered them.

I recall with amazement how much my parents and grandparents knew about the Jewish people of the Bible and their prayers always referred to the God of Abraham, Isaac and Jacob. My goal in researching was to confirm the information I had been given orally. Some of the stories sounded strange and unbelievable, but later it all began to make sense.

They told us that our ancestors had been expelled from Spain and Portugal between 1492 and 1500 because they were non-Catholics. At that time, those Jews were called "New Christians," "Conversos," and "Marranos" (pigs).

Can you imagine how they must have felt when Queen Isabella and King Ferdinand of Spain suddenly announced in 1492 that all Jews must leave the country immediately or be turned over to the feared Spanish Inquisition to be tortured or killed. They were not allowed to take anything of value with them. It was clear that the royal couple wanted an all-Catholic country. Can you imagine if this had happened to you, where would you have gone? What would you have done? How could you have survived without money or goods?

Upon hearing the royal decree, the Jewish people immediately began planning to leave the country. They scattered to other parts of the world where they thought they would be safe. They went to Portugal, Turkey, Holland, Morocco, Greece, France, Italy, England and other parts of the world. Some chose to go even further away to an unknown land, so they headed for the "New World," along with Christopher Columbus. Once they reached the New World, they scattered again throughout North and South America.

It may surprise my readers to learn that in the year 1842 the earliest settlers of the Territory of Colorado were "Sephardic Jews," those who had migrated from Spain and Portugal. "Sephardim" is the Hebrew word for Spain. Many of them were Crypto (secret) Messianic Jews as well. Those were Jews who believed in Yeshua (Jesus) and His teachings.

Thinking about this, I began to wonder was it possible that our family could be the descendants of the early disciples of Jesus Christ that formed the first century church? They were Jews, as well as the later followers who also preached the gospel. Jesus (Yeshua) was a Jew. As a Messianic Jew myself, I had often wondered what happened to all those descendents of the original followers of Jesus. Had all of their descendants died? Did they become what we today call the Christian church? Where would I find the answer to that question?

I began studying the New Testament (New Covenant) scriptures, with the Old Testament (Old Covenant) for background information. Especially promising was my study of the ancient prophets. Many of their prophecies had already been fulfilled and others are still being fulfilled today. I remembered the great promise in Jeremiah:

"Call to me and I will answer you and tell you great and unsearchable things you do not know." (Jeremiah 33: 3) NIV

What a promise! God himself would tell me the great and unsearchable things I did not know.

I had even turned to the research others had already done. I concluded that I still didn't know for sure whether we were, indeed, the offspring of those early followers of Yeshua (Jesus) and the early congregations. I know many generations have past but it is still possible.

I remember reading that through the years, there has always been a remnant of those early followers of Yeshua (Jesus); my ancestors could have possibly been among them. For so many years they had to worship secretly in their homes.

In writing about my family, I decided that I would include only the names of the five generations that have lived during my lifetime. I will do a more extensive genealogical search at a later time and, perhaps, share it in another book.

Any genealogical study should include documentation of the family's DNA, which our study did. It included both my mother's and father's families. It proved the country of origin and eliminated any doubt. Such a study can reveal fascinating facts.

Besides interviews that older family members and friends gave me, I found other valuable sources of information in libraries, courthouses, and government archives, books, newspaper clippings, and magazines. Later, I was able to find sources on the internet. All these sources seemed to support and confirm the earlier information my parents had shared with me.

As my story begins, I hope those who are able to hear God's voice throughout this book will be blessed and come to realize that the Lord God has a purpose and destiny for each and every person. It is also my hope that once this book is released, my family will no longer need to live under a cloud of secrecy. At that time, we will be free to openly shout and sing praises to God for His unwavering faithfulness and protection.

"I will sing of the LORD'S great love forever; with my mouth I will make your faithfulness known through all generations." (Psalm 89: 1) NIV

As a believer, I will "Lift High the Banner," to exalt His wonderful name forever.

Shalom (peace)!

CHAPTER 1

THE BEGINNING: HOW IT ALL STARTED

THE MYSTERY OF THE TEN LOST TRIBES OF ISRAEL

Researching the Tribes
(The Worldwide Scattering)
My Interest in the Tribe of Judah

CHAPTER 1

THE BEGINNING:
HOW IT ALL STARTED

THE MYSTERY

OF THE TEN LOST TRIBES OF ISRAEL

Abraham, Isaac and Jacob are among the most significant men in the Old Testament. I will start my story with Isaac, who was born to Abraham, the Patriarch, and his wife, Sarah, when Abraham was 100 years old and Sarah was 90 years old. The baby was given the name Isaac, which means "laughter," because Sarah laughed when God told her that she would have a baby when she was already old and past the age of childbearing.

"Then God said, 'Yes, but your wife Sarah will bear you a son, and you will call him Isaac. I will establish my covenant with him as an everlasting covenant for his descendants after him.' " (Genesis 17: 19) NIV

"Then the Lord said to Abraham, "Why did Sarah laugh and say, 'Will I really have a child, now that I am old?' Is anything too hard for the Lord? I will return to you at the appointed time next year and Sarah will have a son." (Genesis 18: 13-14) NIV

God kept His promise to Abraham and Sarah because God always keeps His promises. He is faithful. Isaac was the beginning of God's fulfillment of His earlier promise to Abraham that he would be the "... *father of many nations." (Genesis 17: 4), NIV*

Isaac married his first cousin, Rebekah, and, some years later, they had twin sons. They named them Jacob and Esau. Ultimately, God's plan was to be channeled through Jacob, not Esau, even though Esau was the firstborn. More can be learned about the life of Jacob by reading *(Genesis 25-50) NIV.* On one occasion, Jacob wrestled with the angel of the Lord and, when he was victorious, the angel changed his name from Jacob to Israel, after which the land of Israel is named. *(Genesis 32: 26-28) NIV*

God chose the Israelites as His special people. They are children of the covenant and heirs of the promises that God made to Abraham. *(Genesis 12: 1-3) NIV*

Jacob had twelve sons in all and each one became the head of a tribe. The tribe was originally made up of his family and, later on, his descendants. The twelve tribes were Reuben, Simeon, Levi, Judah, Zebulun, Issachar, Dan, Gad, Asher, Naphtali, Joseph and Benjamin.

In recent years, I became fascinated with a study of Israel's twelve tribes. My interest started when I began to research my family's surname (last name), Cordova or Cordoba. I had just finished reading in Genesis about the time when Jacob was nearing the end of his life and wanted to pronounce a blessing over his children. *"And Jacob called unto his sons, and said; Gather yourselves together, that I may tell you that which shall befall you in the last days." (Genesis 49: 1) KJV*

Jacob prophesied to each son about his future. Each was given a description, such as "a fruitful vine," "a doe set free," "a lion's cub" and "a ravenous wolf." Those words and pictures were used to create symbols that would identify each tribe. The symbols were placed on their shields, helmets and individual banners. One had only to see the symbol and he would immediately know which tribe it represented. Even today, it is possible for someone to look at tombstones in old cemeteries and find those belonging to Messianic Jews that have the symbol of a tribe of Israel hidden in the inscription.

The blessing Jacob gave to his son, Judah, was the only one with the mention of royalty:

"The scepter shall not depart from Judah, nor a lawgiver from between his feet, until Shiloh come; and unto him shall the gathering of the people be." *(Genesis 49: 10) KJV*

It is an established fact that the person who was yet to come and to whom the scepter would belong was Yeshua (Jesus), the Messiah. He is an eternal king who rules over an eternal kingdom.

You can imagine my excitement when I realized that my own family's Coat of Arms depicts a lion with a crown on his head and pictures of castles. I also learned that our Coat of Arms was a symbol of the city of Cordoba, Spain. Could it be that we are descendants of the royal line of Judah and of Jesus? What a thought! Even though I was excited, I was also terrified at the thought of the responsibility that would go along with being a part of that royal line. I decided that much more historical research was needed before this could be established; but, it is very interesting.

I began my research again with the period following the death of King Solomon, son of the famous Old Testament King David, who led Israel for 40 years. After King Solomon's death, in approximately 930 B.C., Scripture tell us that because of idolatry and the failure of the Israelites to follow God's laws, their land fell to foreign powers.

God allowed the land of Israel to be split into two separate kingdoms. Ten tribes were known as the Northern Kingdom and the remaining two tribes, Judah and Benjamin, became the Southern Kingdom. There followed a period of turmoil and war, and, eventually, both kingdoms were defeated by their enemies and the people were taken into captivity.

"Therefore the LORD was angry with his people and abhorred his inheritance. He handed them over to the nations, and their foes ruled over them. Their enemies oppressed them and subjected them to their power. Many times He delivered them, but they were bent on rebellion and they wasted away in their sin. But he took note of their distress when he heard their cry; for their sake he remembered his covenant and out of his great love he relented. He caused them to be pitied by all who held them captive." (Psalm 106: 40-46) NIV

After years of captivity, some Jews were given the opportunity to return to their homeland. The two tribes that returned were Judah and

Benjamin of the Southern Kingdom. Today many of them still live in the land of Israel. The other ten tribes of the Northern Kingdom chose not to return to their homeland. Instead, they were scattered throughout the world and are known today as the "Ten Lost Tribes of Israel."

This presented me with a quandary. How could my forefathers have been both a part of the tribe of Judah that settled in Israel, as well as a part of the tribes that scattered throughout the nations? I knew that my forefathers had migrated from Israel to Spain and then, eventually, to Southeastern Colorado, where they were among the earliest settlers in the Territory. I began to research the matter further and discovered that people had begun leaving Israel very early in history.

A big migration occurred to the land we know as Spain. The country was known to ancient Greeks as Iberia and to Romans as Hispania. It was appealing because of its many natural resources. Maybe my forefathers returned from captivity to settle in the land of Israel, then migrated to Spain and, finally, to America. Jonathan Bernis, states in his article entitled "The Scattering of the Tribes of Israel," in <u>Jewish Voice Today</u>, March/April 2005 Edition:

> "*Today we find that there are around 6 million Jews living in Israel—but there are physical descendents of Abraham, Isaac, and Jacob dwelling in almost every nation on the planet. In fact, there are estimates that the total dispersed Jewish population is anywhere from 20 to 30 million!*"

As you can image, the tribes that scattered eventually became integrated with other cultures through intermarriage to the degree that today many Jews no longer know to which tribe they belong. Even more surprising, some may not even realize that they are Jews. As I mentioned earlier, we call the ten tribes that were scattered the "Ten Lost Tribes of Israel."

It is my hope that one day every Jew will be able to identify his own tribe and know that he has never been "lost" in the eyes of God.

Bernis, Jonathan. "What Happened to the Lost Tribes of Israel? The Scattering of the Tribes of Israel." <u>Jewish Voice Today</u> [Up Front] March/April 2005.

CHAPTER 2

THE GREAT MIGRATION

SEPHARDIC JEWS, COLORADO'S

EARLIEST SETTLERS

(Migration Caused by Religious Persecution)

CHAPTER 2

THE GREAT MIGRATION

My story began long before my family left Europe to come to the United States. According to history, it is possible that my family was part of a group that left the *"Eretz of Israel,"* Land of Israel, as early as 70 A.D. and migrated to Spain (Sepharad), where they lived as exiles. *(Obadiah 1: 20) KJV*

I researched the history of Spain and found that people were constantly leaving Israel to go to Spain in search of a better life. Spain was a country that had great mines, yielding much silver and gold. It was a well-known fact.

Still, I don't know the actual reason why my ancestors left Israel and migrated to Spain.

However, when I think about it, they may have been members of one of the first century churches of Yeshua (Jesus) and His disciples. They may also have been afraid of the persecution those churches were experiencing in Israel. We know today that all of the Old Testament prophets were eventually killed, and, later, Jesus and his disciples.

Centuries later, all residents of Spain were required by the royal family to convert to Catholicism because they wanted an all Catholic country. Those who refused to convert were turned over to The Spanish Inquisition for torture or death. I understand many families obeyed the royal edict, but did so in name only. They secretly continued to observe their Jewish traditions.

Unfortunately, it wasn't long before their Catholic neighbors discovered that they were still observing Jewish traditions. They were also studying both the Old and New Testaments of the Bible, a practice forbidden by the Catholic Church at that time. They began calling those Jews *"New Christians," "Conversos,"* or *"Marranos,"* the Spanish word for "pigs." Most Catholics hated Jews anyway because they blamed them for the death of Jesus. As a result, no Jews were welcome in society.

By 1371, all Jewish citizens were forced to live under severe restrictions. They were required to wear a humiliating yellow badge that singled them out in public and they could not have any personal or business dealings with members of the Catholic Church. They were allowed to engage only in limited occupations and were heavily taxed. They were taxed not only by the King, but also by the Archbishops of the Roman Catholic Church. On top of the official taxes, they had to pay taxes on meat and wine to their local Jewish government for the support of religious and educational institutions in the community.

The Spanish Inquisition

Not only the Marranos, but many who were non-Jewish, were accused simply for doing something that appeared Jewish in nature. Official Inquisition spies called "Confidants" were everywhere. Although punishments given out by the Inquisition varied, two common practices were the confiscation of property and burning of the offender at the stake. Because the Catholic Church didn't want to be held responsible for the shedding of blood, the condemned were turned over to the civil authorities to carry out the death sentence.

A network of prisons was set up. Informers everywhere were ready to turn in a neighbor, business rival or even a relative, whether guilty or not. Sometimes a prisoner had a short wait for a trial and sometimes not. However, the outcome was almost never in doubt. Very few went free.

Torture was used as a tool for extracting confessions. Water torture, the thumbscrew and the rack were used to extract confessions from the innocent, as well as from the guilty. Even if a prisoner had done nothing wrong, weeks and months of painful torture often resulted in a "confession."

According to one historical source, the Spanish Inquisition handled over 300,000 cases and sentenced at least 30,000 people to death.

The Great Migration

Within a three-week period in the spring of 1492, King Ferdinand and Queen Isabella of Spain issued two seemingly unrelated, but fateful decrees. In the first, issued on March 31, 1492, the royal couple ordered all Jews to leave Spanish soil within four months. They could take nothing of value with them. The second edict, on April 17, bestowed the exalted title "Admiral of the Ocean Sea" upon a persistent Genoese sailor, Christopher Columbus, and directed him to undertake an expedition in search of a new route to the rich Indies.

Finally, on August 2, 1492, more than 300,000 Jews were expelled from Spain. They scattered throughout the world. As Christopher Columbus and his crew sailed out of the harbor at Palos, Spain, undoubtedly they passed other ships carrying Jews away from the land that had been their home for centuries.

The Jews that left Spain became known as Sephardic Jews. Some of them migrated to the New World, and, I believe, from the oral history passed down in my family, that my mother's and father's ancestors may have been part of that group. From that point forward in my research, I came to depend on oral history from older family members and their close friends.

I found through my research my mother's ancestors had entered the country through a port in Louisiana. From there, they traveled to New Iberia, Louisiana, then Natchitoches, Texas, then to Nacogdoches, Texas, and, finally, to Colorado.

My father's ancestors landed at a port in Galveston, Texas, then went to Nacogdoches, Texas, and perhaps Waco, Texas, then finally to Colorado. I found my family's surnames on Passenger Lists of Arrivals at both ports, as well as a port in New York. I don't know for certain whether any of those passengers were family members, but they could have been, since the name is still very common in those areas.

I have also located their surnames in an early Census of Texas. The information family members gave me was rather difficult to follow, as there were few written records. However, it does make sense. Their migration from Europe continued on to New Mexico and Colorado, where they finally settled.

My research also revealed that many groups from 1492 through the 1500's scattered into other parts of the world, including Argentina and other South American countries.

My ancestors possessed very few books, but those they had were written in the 15th century Judaeo-Spanish "Ladino" language common to Spain. Because they were the first settlers in the Territories of Colorado and New Mexico, they brought the Ladino (Old Castilian) language with them. It immediately became the primary language spoken in the remote areas where they settled. The only book in the Ladino language that I have ever personally seen was a Bible owned by our pastor's family. It is speculated that Christopher Columbus might have spoken Ladino also. It wasn't until many years later, when some of the young men from Colorado went into the Armed Forces of the United States that they realized the uniqueness of the Ladino language.

The expulsion from Spain was not the only experience of its kind for the Jewish people. Rooted in Jewish history is a long and sad tradition of forced movements. At one time, the Jews had a land of their own, called Canaan, Israel, Palestine or the Holy Land. That piece of land has had an importance to Jews that is not only historical, but religious and emotional as well. Even when physically separated from the land, whether for a short or long period of time, Jews have never allowed themselves to forget their ancient homeland.

Because of the continued disobedience of the Jews over the centuries, there began a period of punishment when God was silent for 400 years. At the end of that time, God spoke to His people again when He introduced a New Covenant (New Testament). That was when Yeshua (Jesus), the anointed one and only begotten Son of God, was born as a fulfillment of Old Testament prophecies. His mission in life was to restore man's broken relationship with God the Father.

The entire life of Jesus had been prophesied about before He was born. His ministry on earth had been described in detail, as well as His sacrificial death on the (tree) cross, so that all those who accepted Jesus as their Lord and Savior could be forgiven of their sins and restored to fellowship with God.

In the New Covenant, (Yeshua) Jesus promised to come and make His dwelling with us, as well as within us. Putting His Laws in our minds, and would write them in our hearts. This is a promise to all those who would trust Him. He would be their Lord and they would be His people.

*"For if that first **covenant** had been faultless, and then should no place have been sought for the second. For finding fault with them, he saith, Behold, the days come, saith the Lord, when I will make a new covenant with the house of Israel and with the house of Judah:*

Not according to the covenant that I made with their fathers in the day when I took them by the hand to lead them out of the land of Egypt; because they continued not in my covenant, and I regarded them not, saith the Lord.

*For this **is** the covenant that I will make with the house of Israel after those days, saith the Lord; I will put my laws into their mind, and write them in their hearts: and I will be to them a God, and they shall be to me a people:" (Hebrews 8: 7-10) KJV* See also *(Hebrews 9: 11-15, 22-28) KJV and (Hebrews 10:12-17) KJV.*

The entire Bible was written by Jewish men under the inspiration of the Holy Spirit.

My parents believed that most of the Old Testament prophecies given by Isaiah, Daniel, Jeremiah, Amos and Hosea about the Jewish Messiah, as well as some other prophets, have already been fulfilled. They also believed that other prophecies dealing with future events would be fulfilled very soon.

The truth I will emphasize throughout this book will be the importance of the life of Yeshua (Jesus). For the most part, historians have simply ignored the fact that the birth of Yeshua (Jesus) was the fulfillment of Old Testament prophecies about the promised Jewish Messiah. It was

His birth, life, death and resurrection that laid the foundation for today's believers.

I will relate to my readers what was told to us children by my parents. What is special about my early childhood is that my parents told us all they could about Yeshua (Jesus). It seems to me that today few Jewish parents believe in Jesus as their Messiah, so they don't tell their children about Jesus.

I knew from a very early age that one day I would be privileged to share this story with others. I also believe that the Lord inspired me to tell that one day this secret about our belief in Jesus could be revealed. It has been my privilege and honor to reveal it to you this day.

SEPHARDIC JEWS,

COLORADO'S EARLIEST SETTLERS

The Spanish explorers who came to Colorado in the 1500's in search of gold were the first white men to visit the area. When they failed to find gold, they left. Years later, the Spanish came again. This time they decided to settle there. That's when they discovered that the Arapaho, Cheyenne, Comanche, Kiowa, Pawnee and Ute Indian tribes were already living there. History tells us that the Spaniards decided they should try to civilize the Indians and convert them to Christianity, so they started constructing villages for them to live in. Unfortunately, the Indians rejected their efforts. The Indian problem was one of the main reasons why permanent settlements weren't established until the middle of the nineteenth century.

Permanent Settlements

In early 1858, several families of Sephardic Jews migrated from Europe (Spain and Portugal) into Taos, New Mexico. There they were able to live peacefully alongside the Pueblo Indians. Those Indians were descended from the early Anasazi Indians, which had one of the most highly developed civilizations in North America. They lived in compact, terraced structures called pueblos. Their tribal name, "Pueblo," came from the Spanish word for village. They and their ancestors had lived in the Taos Valley of New Mexico for over two hundred years.

The Pueblo Indians had welcomed the settlers. Many of their Indian women became household helpers, especially when someone was sick. They were knowledgeable about natural herbs and cures. Also, when the few single men and women among the settlers were unable to find a spouse among their own people, they sometimes intermarried with the Indians.

Later, the Taos settlers moved once again to the Territory of Colorado and settled in what is now known as the Huerfano and Las Animas Counties of Southeastern Colorado. They became the first permanent settlers in the area. They named their village *La Plaza de los Leones*, meaning "Town of the Lions." In an article, I read that the name of the village may have been the surname of a family named "Leon." Later, it was renamed Walsenburg, in honor of a German merchant and community leader named Fred Walsen.

The Taos settlers arrived in covered wagons loaded with merchandise, household items and other belongings. They brought with them horses, mules, cattle, sheep, goats, pigs and chickens. To reach the area, they had to cross a dangerous mountain pass today called Raton Pass. As soon as they entered the Territory of Colorado, they quickly realized there were hostile Indians already living there. Those Indians were direct descendants of prehistoric tribes.

There was plenty of distrust on both sides. As a result, the settlers took extensive measures to protect themselves from Indian attacks and wild animals. They started building homes and arranging them in the shape of a U, with only one opening. That way, the center of the settlement was somewhat enclosed and protected. Each settlement was named for a prominent family member or leader. Many settlements were started beside rivers, such as Purgatory, the Indian name for the river. Later, the settlements grew into villages, and, later still, coal mining camps. Then various geographical areas were given county names. The population continued to grow as people came from other states and countries. At one time there were 88 different languages spoken in the Territory.

There were two factors that encouraged growth in the region. The first was when the government began offering free land grants to those willing to relocate to Colorado. That attracted a second group of Sephardic Jews from the Taos mountain area of Northern New Mexico. This second group settled in The Sangre de Cristo Mountains ("Blood of Christ"), an area which was part of the Colorado Mountains and of the Maxwell Land Grant. In that group were ranchers, merchants, farmers and soldiers. As you can imagine, they were extremely excited about the opportunity to become land owners.

The second factor was when the Atchison, Topeka & Santa Fe Railroad began expanding to the west in 1860. That really opened the doors to adventurous newcomers from the East coast.

My research about that period of Colorado history led me to look into early steamship passenger lists and dates of entry into America from Europe in order to determine my ancestors' original point of entry into the country. I learned that many of the settlers from Taos were Sephardic Jews (or Sephardim, the Hebrew name for Spain), whose ancestors had fled from Spain in order to escape religious persecution and the murderous Spanish Inquisition. Even after the families that migrated to the Southwestern United States had arrived there, they still continued to fear the long arm of The Inquisition. Many generations later, their fear was somewhat diminished once they were able to assimilate into the fast growing population.

However, there were still pockets of persecutions from neighbors who knew them, so that fear had become a genuine fear, justified or not, of what might happen if their secret was discovered. Fear became fear in itself, to the degree that some even rejected their Jewish heritage completely, and refused to discuss the subject.

The winter weather in the Colorado Mountains was so harsh that people who lived there sometimes wondered whether they could survive another winter with many months so long and harsh. The settlers and the Indians had two things in common. They both had suffered many hardships in the past and they both had learned how to survive in a bitterly cold climate.

The settlers were a hardworking, industrious people, who cleared the land and made it livable in the shortest possible time. Their first houses were constructed of logs, but later on they were built from sun-dried bricks and called "adobe." I learned that this was an ancient Middle Eastern art of building houses, which caught on very rapidly in the Colorado Territory. Each home was designed with a certain number of bricks that were made of clay, mud, straw and water. The clay mixture was placed into a wooden form that ensured the bricks would be uniform in size. Then they had to be completely dried before the foundation could be set, so they were placed in the sun for a period of time. The family would plan the size of their house and then the bricks would be made.

Once the foundation was set, the building of the walls could begin. On the outside walls, each row of bricks was measured and checked with a plumb line to make sure that it was straight. The walls were several inches thick, which kept the house cool in the summer and warm in the winter. Finally, logs were used to construct the roof and then a layer of sod was placed on top of the house for insulation. Because of the ample supply of both sun and rain in the area, plants could be grown on the roofs in the early summer which helped to keep it cool inside. The adobe houses proved to be very satisfactory for the area. They were so reliable that some of the ruins still stand today, even if they have been empty and isolated for years.

Settlers usually built their houses and barns on their land (ranches) first. Next, they built a church or worship center, post office, schoolhouse for the children and buildings for the merchants.

By 1860, as the settlers' families became more self-sufficient, they were also expected to make some kind of contribution to the welfare of the community. To accomplish that, they shared produce from their gardens and byproducts from their sheep, goats, cattle and poultry.

Most men were good hunters and provided meat for their families. Some of them worked on the larger ranches were they sheared sheep to make wool clothing and cured leather to make shoes. The women also helped to provide for their families. They became skilled in the culinary arts as they fed their families, workers and guests. They prepared special meals for religious holidays. They sewed, washed and repaired their clothes, made soap, raised and taught children, grew edible herbs for medicinal purposes and some of the women became midwives so babies could be brought safely into the world.

They established routines for each day of the week. For example, Monday would be laundry day, Tuesday was ironing day, Wednesday was sewing day, Thursday was housecleaning day and Friday was the cooking day. That was when food was prepared for company or for a religious holiday. That included baking bread and preparing food to be eaten by the congregation after church services.

In my family, Saturdays were religious days and Sundays were days set aside for spiritual training, either at home or at church. That was when the children in our family were taught good manners and respect for the elderly. Sometimes our Sunday church services began a "Revival," which could last several days. Those Revivals were very special.

Most families knew how to pray about their problems and needs; they asked God for His guidance and protection. They also read and studied the Scriptures regularly.

At a very young age, the children in my family were required to help with household chores. As we grew older, we also helped outside on the ranch, in the garden and with the animals.

Many generations later, in spite of numerous hardships and lingering fears of the religious persecution they had suffered earlier, my ancestors and other early settlers lived relatively comfortable lives, as they paved the way for future generations that would one day populate the beautiful State of Colorado.

CHAPTER 3

INTRODUCTION TO THE FAMILY

Daddy's Story

Mama's story

Celebration of life

My musical Heritage

Names, Names, and more Names

Circle of Love: Memories of Family Meals

"I Can Only Imagine . . . Being an Only Child"

The tree Grows and the Branches Become Many

CHAPTER 3

INTRODUCTION TO THE FAMILY:

Daddy's story-Mama's story

Daddy and Mama, 1929.

JOSEPH D. CORDOVA, and
JENNIE (WOODSON/APODACA) CORDOVA

CHAPTER 3

INTRODUCTION TO THE FAMILY

Daddy's Story—Mama's Story

My Daddy's story reminds me of the Old Testament scriptures concerning the Jewish patriarch, Abram (Abraham), who was chosen by God to be the "Father of Many Nations," including Israel.

It was because of Abram's close personal relationship with God that he was chosen for this special blessing. The Bible states:

"Now the Lord had said unto Abram, get thee out of thy country, and from thy kindred, and from thy father's house, unto a land that I will show thee:

And I will make of thee a great nation, and I will bless thee, and make thy name great; and thou shalt be a blessing:

And I will bless them that bless thee, and curse him that curseth thee: and in thee shall all families of the earth be blessed." (Genesis 12: 1-3) KJV

The Bible also states that God blesses men and women who believe in His Word, the Bible, and who are obedient to Him.

My ancestors agreed with the fundamental beliefs of the early Christian congregations, which included the worship of ONE GOD and the acceptance of Yeshua (Jesus Christ, the Anointed One) as their Messiah.

Therefore, the worship of man-made statues, images, other gods, including church Saints was considered to be idol worship, according to the Ten Commandments. Those early believers were called "Messianic Jews."

Somehow, over the years, Daddy had totally drifted away from his religious roots and it wasn't until he married my Mother that he returned to the faith of his ancestors.

Those beliefs were not popular and placed him in direct conflict with the religious practices of the community and even some of our extended family members who had intermarried with people of other faiths. Those relatives were very offended when Daddy tried to show them in the Bible that God forbids us to worship any religious idols, statues or images. *(Exodus 20: 1-5); (Psalm 115: 3-8) KJV*

By God's grace, my Father was later called into the ministry. From that time forward, he went about sharing the good news of Jesus with everyone who would listen. Because his message was not accepted by everyone in the family or community, he experienced religious persecution. Nevertheless, Daddy continued to preach the gospel message during the remainder of his life. You will learn more about my parents as you read the following biographies. Through their godly lives and their steadfast devotion to God, our entire family was blessed, just as God had blessed Abraham. As a result, most of their children and grandchildren have accepted the Messianic belief that Yeshua (Jesus) is their Messiah.

CHAPTER 3

DADDY'S STORY

Joseph Delfin Cordova

1892-1968

My Daddy, Joseph D. Cordova, was born August 31, 1892, in Mora County, in northern, New Mexico, of Sephardic Jewish parents. His father, Joseph Gregory Cordova, and his mother, Julia Ann (Rael) Cordova, my grandparents, were both born in 1871. Daddy was their firstborn son. My father's sister, Emma, was born November 24, 1893, and his brother, Rosendo "Ross," was born February 6, 1897. My Daddy's grandparents were born in the 1820's. They were all born in the same area of New Mexico (in the vicinity of Taos).

In 1898, when Daddy was six years old, his 27-year-old mother became sick and died of unknown causes. Two years later, in 1900, his 29-year-old father also died of unknown causes. Daddy was eight, Emma was seven and Ross was only three years old. The children were orphaned at a very early age. They were placed in the homes of their relatives, who were the second generation of the earliest settlers of Colorado. Emma went to live with her grandmother, while the two boys were placed with an uncle and aunt who lived on a ranch and had older children of their own. Unlike the boys, Emma had a very happy childhood and upbringing.

The boys were small and when they arrived at their uncle and aunt's home, they were given the job of caring for the sheep. Their uncle felt this would be a good way to start them out working on the ranch. It was not unusual for children of the early settlers to be given this responsibility as soon as they were old enough. Some families owned as many as a thousand sheep.

Since Daddy was the oldest, his uncle thought that he could begin taking care of the sheep alone until his brother, Ross, was old enough to join him. So he sent him out into the pasture alone, with little adult supervision. His uncle was right and Daddy did the job by himself until his brother, Ross, was old enough to help him. Even so, it was a lonely job for two little boys.

The family had limited resources and Daddy remembered being sent to work without much food. He was strong-willed and very resourceful even at that tender age. Once he killed the smallest lamb in the flock and they roasted it over an open fire. This satisfied their hunger, but created another problem for them. The smell of roasting lamb drew coyotes, wolves and wild dogs. The animals tried to attack the boys and the flock in an attempt to get to the roasting lamb. They ended up taking some of it. However, from the beginning, the boys realized that it would be dangerous, but they felt it was worth the risk. They learned to appreciate that special meal since they couldn't have another one like it.

It is difficult to imagine all that the young brothers went through, but times were very hard in the early 1900's. When Daddy told us the story about caring for the sheep, we would think of King David in the Bible. As a young child, King David was also a shepherd and God's constant protection was with him. God blessed and cared for Daddy and Ross in the same way.

When the boys weren't taking care of the flock, they were still required to help around the ranch. They learned to do many farming and ranching jobs. It seemed that they were worked much harder than their uncle's older sons and they began to feel mistreated. Daddy even developed bitterness toward his uncle. The boys made the decision to leave the ranch as soon as they were old enough to care for themselves. When Daddy was fifteen years old, he decided to go ahead and leave; but it was agreed that he would return for Ross later. It was years before Daddy could completely forgive his uncle.

As agreed, when Ross was older, Daddy returned to the ranch for him. They left the ranch and joined a caravan of families who were traveling to Colorado. The brothers realized that it would be a long and difficult trip, but they were anxious to start over in a new place. The families took with them food, supplies, animals and whatever else they felt they needed to start a new life. They shared all the food and chores.

As expected, the trip was a difficult one. Daddy recalled how the covered wagons were placed in a circle at night to keep out wild animals and unfriendly Indians. Then the people moved inside the circle for protection. That's when they prepared their food for the next day. They tried to go to bed early so that they could leave again at daybreak.

A New Life

Once the caravan reached Colorado, the boys were quickly able to find work. By then they were experienced ranch hands, cowboys and day laborers. They could do almost any odd job. When they were older, they worked in the coal mines. They also learned the craft of carpentry. At one time, Daddy became a merchant and sold clothing. He enjoyed selling, but he didn't like staying indoors. Eventually, he became restless, so both brothers began working in construction, which became their favorite occupation. Each of them was definitely a "Jack-of-all-Trades" and they worked very hard.

About 1912, Daddy met a Sephardic Jewish farmer named J. L. Bargas. It is likely that he was employed by him as a farmhand, for that is when he met J. L.'s beautiful daughter, Antonia "Tonie." They soon began dating and it wasn't long before Tonie and Daddy were married. At that point, Daddy was finally able to settle down and find purpose for his life. Years later, his sister, Emma, married Toni's brother, Gabriel.

Daddy and Tonie had two daughters: Umatilla (1915-1929) and Alyce (1920-1991). In 1922, when the daughters were still quite small, Tonie became very ill with tuberculosis and died at the age of twenty-four. Once again, Daddy faced the painful death of a loved one. He immediately began looking for relatives willing to care for his daughters while he worked. Unfortunately, most relatives already had children of their own and some had very large families.

Then the unexpected happened. Seven-year-old Umatilla, who was exposed to her mother's highly contagious tuberculosis, had to be placed in a medical institution in Denver. Her maternal grandmother was living in Denver at the time, so she was able to visit Umatilla often.

Also, Daddy was able to find work in Denver, which enabled him to help take care of his sick daughter. He planned to bring Umatilla home just as soon as the doctors said that she was well. That hope turned into a huge disappointment because Umatilla's tuberculosis progressed to the point that she was never again allowed to return home. There was an epidemic of tuberculosis at the time that left many families broken and desolate. Umatilla died in 1929 at the young age of fourteen.

Her sister, Alyce, was only two years old when their mother died. Even though Alyce had also been exposed to her mother's tuberculosis, fortunately, she did not catch the terrible disease that took both her mother and sister. While Daddy continued to work, Alyce was sent to live with relatives. She developed into a healthy and very strong-willed child. When she reached school age, she was placed in a Catholic boarding school in Denver. It's not surprising that when Alyce was an adult, she remembered nothing about her mother and very little about her sister.

Another Beginning

In 1929, not long after the death of Tonie, Daddy met and married my mother, Jennie Woodson Apodaca. They immediately agreed to bring Alyce home from Catholic school. By that time, Alyce was nine years old. Mama and Alyce were very close to the same age, so they felt more like sisters than mother and stepdaughter. Alyce always said that when God made Mama, He used a very special pattern and then retired the pattern. She believed that Mama was the sweetest, kindest person in the entire world. She lived with Mama and Daddy until she was married in 1937.

Soon after Mama and Daddy married, the family began to grow. Together they had fifteen children: Marian Holley/Jordan; Julie Marlow;

Priscilla Parton; David Pete; Ernestine Ingram; Sarah Yoder; Leroy; Daniel; Freddy; Joseph Del; Evelyn Ellis/Archuleta; Richard; Eva Rogers; Edna Hemsoth and Betsy Barta/Gladieux.

At one time when we were children, our family lived on a ranch in the small community of Augusta, Colorado, where Daddy made sure that we all learned how to work hard. He always said "that's what children are for." The farm was a very busy place, with many chores to be done, especially during the spring and summer seasons.

Sometimes Mama would let the girls play with homemade paper dolls cut out from the Sears Catalog. When she would see Daddy in the distance driving toward home, she would quickly give each girl a job to do . . . mending, crocheting, sweeping, mopping or anything else . . . before he reached the house; because he expected us always to be working.

In the springtime, Daddy would plant our vegetable garden and other crops that required watering by way of a community irrigation ditch that was shared by all the ranchers in the area. To prevent water from overflowing the ditch and flooding our crops, Daddy had to monitor the system very closely. Each family was assigned a certain day of the week when it could water their crops. I can still visualize Daddy in his big rubber boots, with a hoe on his shoulder, monitoring the water flow.

Sometimes in the summer months, when Daddy was out in the fields or had gone into town, the children would sneak out to go swimming. There was a watering tank at the windmill, where the horses and cows drank, that made a perfect "swimming pool." Once we were sure all the animals were out in the field and Daddy was away, we would swim and play in the watering tank until we saw him coming home. Quickly, we would wipe down the tank, jump out of the water and rush back to the house so that he would think we had been working hard the whole time he was gone.

Autumn was the time for harvesting the oats, alfalfa hay, wheat and rye. It was another busy time of the year. Since the oldest children were girls and not yet strong enough to work in the fields, Daddy had to depend on his oldest son, David, and other hired hands to bring in the harvest. This meant there would be extra mouths to feed. Mama always had the meals ready for them on time. When the meal was ready, she would ring the dinner bell and Daddy would require the workmen to wash their hands outside in a special place before they could come into the house to eat.

The girls were given the chores of rounding up the cows, feeding and milking them. They also had to feed the horses, chickens, guinea hens, pigs, dogs and cats.

Daddy's Memories

Sometimes Daddy would tell us about his early years on the ranch and he would shed a few tears over the memories.

He also shared with us what he could remember about his natural parents. One of the most important memories to him was the special blessing each of his parents gave to him and his siblings on their deathbed. It was an ancient Jewish blessing (*Brakhak*). Daddy remembered how sad his beautiful mother (my grandmother) looked when she realized that she would soon be leaving the children she dearly loved. In that situation, it seemed that an early death at twenty-seven years was very unfair.

Two years later, when their father (my grandfather) was on his deathbed, he also gave his three children the *Brakhak* blessing. He realized that his children would soon become orphans and that life would be very difficult for them.

By His Grace

Since Daddy had to work so hard when he was a child, he didn't get much of a formal education. But, with Mama's help, he learned to read and write and he taught himself math. He also began to study the Bible extensively and that is when he became a believer in Yeshua (Jesus Christ, the Messiah). When their first child was born, Daddy realized that he was being given an opportunity to pass his faith on to that child and to any other children they might have.

By God's grace, he was healed of much of his earlier emotional suffering. It was at that time when he completely forgave his uncle and became a very joyous and loving person. He adored his family.

Eventually, Daddy became an ordained minister of the Gospel. For several years he was the pastor of a small congregation in the community where we lived. Later he preached to other congregations in the surrounding area. Daddy believed in the Old Testament (Old Covenant), which was the first covenant between God and the Jewish patriarch, Abraham. Because of Abraham's faith and obedience, he would become the father of many nations. So, in that sense, Abraham was the beginning of the Jewish nation. The practice of circumcision was a symbol of the Old Covenant and was required of all Jewish males.

Through the prophet, Moses, God gave His people commandments by which to live. However, they failed in their efforts to keep God's commandments; and, because of their disobedience, God was silent for 400 years. At the end of that time, God made a New Covenant (New Testament) with the Jewish people in order to restore their fellowship with Him. He sent His son, Jesus, to die for their sins and stated that whosoever believed in Him as the Son of God would be saved and have eternal life. Jesus is the "bridge" that connects the Old and New Testaments of the Bible.

It is through the birth, life, death, burial and resurrection of Jesus that all mankind (Jews and Gentiles alike) can be restored to Fellowship with God. It is the responsibility of the Holy Ghost to teach us spiritual truths and how to live for God.

Family worship was very important to Daddy. In his opinion, there was no acceptable excuse for missing church. He wanted his entire family in church for every service. We had to set a good example or else he would declare, "I will not preach."

He was blessed with Godly wisdom and he gave God credit for all of his blessings. He was often seen walking around, praising and thanking God. He loved the Lord and expressed that love even more in his later years.

Other Talents

Daddy had a brilliant mind. He invented many things that he used on the farm. He didn't apply for a patent on any of them simply because he didn't think it was important. If it served his purpose at the time, that was all he wanted and needed.

He was good in mathematics and had great musical talent as well. He built a violin from scratch, not from a kit. He created every part of it from purchased raw materials. It was a labor of love and the finished violin gave out a clear and beautiful sound. It looked very professional. He also made a guitar and banjo from scratch.

Daddy played several musical instruments by ear and his favorite instrument was the violin. He would play it for the congregation during church services. He came from a long line of musicians. His father and grandfather also had played the violin. The 1880 census listed his grandfather's occupation as "musician."

Music was good therapy for him. In the evenings, he devoted his spare time to playing various instruments and worshiping God. He passed his love for music onto his children and grandchildren. Even today many of us play musical instruments.

Daddy's Grandmother

His grandmother, whom he called "Nana," was listed in the 1880 census as a seamstress. Daddy said she was always a very hard worker. Her nationality was listed as Native American, but the name of her tribe was omitted. Daddy's mother and the rest of the women in the family inherited her love for sewing.

Nana seemed to know exactly what to do to help other families when they were sick. Neighbors frequently came to her for medical advice. She knew all about the healing properties of herbs and roots. She not only had many children of her own, but she took in other children who had been orphaned. When her family moved from Taos, New Mexico, to Colorado, they were among the first settlers in the area.

In her day, hostile nomadic Indians would kidnap white women and children and sell them as servants to other Indian tribes or non-Indians. They would also kidnap Indian women and children from faraway tribes and sell them to local Indian tribes or to Spaniards who lived in the area. This happened quite often.

They would also raid the homes of the settlers when they thought no one was at home. Usually, however, the family would see them coming and would hide in the cellar. The Indians would ransack the house for food, blankets, guns and whatever else they could find while the family huddled in the cellar.

In fact, Daddy told us that his own grandfather, who was old and blind, would hear the Indians' horses as they were coming and would tell the family to quickly hide in the secret cellar under the rug on the kitchen floor. When the Indians arrived, he would be sitting by the door of their home with his white cane, silently praying for God's protection. They didn't harm him because he appeared to be an old, helpless man living alone. They would take whatever they wanted and leave. It was only because of their enormous faith in God that the early settlers survived those dangerous times.

Daddy

Daddy's Mother
and baby sister Emma

Daddy and Mama, 1959

MAMA'S STORY

Jennie Odelia (Woodson/Apodaca/Cordova)

Jennie Odelia was born in a small community near Gardner, Colorado, on April 10, 1914. She was the youngest child of Peter "Pete" Woodson/Apodaca and Manulita "Mable" Lopes, who were married November 20, 1896, in Creston, Colorado. Pete Woodson/Apodaca was born September 6, 1872, in Saguache, Colorado, and died December 13, 1945. "Mable" Lopes/Apodaca was born January 1, 1880, in Gardner, Colorado, and died June 26, 1963.

The name "Lopes" is a Portuguese name that rhymes with "ropes." Manulita was a name given to Jennie's mother by a Catholic friend of the family because Manulita was born the first day of January. Children born on the first day of January were traditionally named Emmanuel, if male, and Manulita, if female. The name represents the Catholic Patron Saint for January the first.

Together they had four children. Victoria was born in 1898, died in 1972; Adolph was born in 1904, died in 2001; Dora was born in 1906, was 105 in 2011, and still lives in California today; Jennie was born in 1914, and was 97 in 2011. She still lives in Colorado today.

Jennie's father, Peter, was adopted when he was about five years old. I have not been able to find out much about his birth family until recently. He grew up in the household of James Bernard Woodson and Julia Ann (Vigil) Woodson. James was born February 3, 1820, in Virginia, and Julia was born February 24, 1843, in New Mexico.

The 1880 Colorado Federal Census listed Peter Woodson, age eight, as living in the Woodson family household in Saguache, Colorado. It wasn't until 1894, four years after his foster father died, that Peter learned he had been adopted. He also learned that he was the natural son of an Italian man named Joseph John Apodaca and Jennie (Martinez) Apodaca. Peter was unable to find out anything else about them; but, since then, my brother, Del, learned that Jennie Martinez was Joseph J. Apodaca's second wife.

With this information, I went back to our family records to see if I could learn anything more. I did find a Certificate of Baptism at Saint Mary's Catholic Church in Walsenburg, Colorado. This gave Peter Apodaca's correct birth date, which was the same one he had used all his life. It also gave the names of his parents. Even later census reports were not helpful.

When Peter was a young man, he had several outdoor occupations, including sheepherding. In the early days, sheepherding was one of the jobs usually assigned to a youngster in the family. The Woodson family had thousands of sheep and their farm was one of the largest in the area.

Julia Woodson was widowed on December 13, 1894, and remarried on December 25, 1895, to her husband's long-time friend and business partner, John Lawrence. It seemed to be a marriage of convenience. In Mr. Lawrence's diary, he admitted that he continued to call his wife "Mrs. Woodson," never "Mrs. Lawrence" or "Julia." As a result of their marriage, Mr. Lawrence became the overseer of the large Woodson farm and property. At that time, the family included Peter, Orville and Myrtle Phillips, the adopted children of John Lawrence, and Julia's brother, Daniel Vigil. They had a very large house.

Even though this was Peter's childhood home, when Julia Woodson remarried, Peter moved out. When he was grown, he never talked about it. It may have been too painful for him to remember. Julia died November 3, 1901. She and both of her husbands are buried in Hillside Cemetery in Saguache, Colorado.

My mother's father, Peter (Pete), had hazel eyes and both he and his son, Adolph, were tall. Victoria and Dora had brown eyes, while Jennie and Adolph inherited their mother's blue eyes. In fact, all of their mother's family had blue eyes. It's likely that Jennie got her love for reading and writing from her father. He always enjoyed studying the Bible.

Peter was educated in Saguache schools and records there said that he was a good student. He had beautiful penmanship in a very ornate style. In his diary, John Lawrence, Peter's stepfather, said that Peter was an excellent speller and was good in mathematics.

Peter loved nature and, when he married Manulita on November 20, 1896, he bought a farm in the beautiful Colorado Mountains. There was a great deal of work to be done on the farm, so he was required to do many different jobs.

His love for the outdoors caused Peter, at one time, to become a lumberjack. He would often take Jennie and Manulita to the forest where he was working. Jennie has many pleasant memories of those beautiful mountains, and, especially, of the different animals and insects she observed during their visits there. She remembers how nice and quiet it was, with only the sound of falling trees in the distance.

Jennie spent her early childhood living with her parents at their home in Saguache, Huerfano County, Colorado. Her father lived there his entire life. The name Saguache is an Indian name meaning "blue earth."

Jennie recalls her father as a very caring person. He loved music and couldn't contain himself whenever he heard polka music playing. His feet just "went to dancing."

Jennie's mother, Manulita, was a beautiful, loving woman. She did chores both inside and outside of the house, while her husband worked in the forest. She enjoyed doing laundry for her neighbors and liked ironing clothes. She also loved to bake and was known for the fried meat pies that she baked, especially for holidays. She was very talented in crafts and made many gifts for her family. She crocheted pillow cases and trimmed them with beautiful laces. She taught Jennie and her sisters how to sew and weave colorful rugs.

Jennie's sisters and brother were older than she was, so they left home when she was still young. Later on, Jennie and her family moved to Aguilar, Colorado, and lived there for several years.

Then they moved to Trinidad, Colorado, where they built a home with their own hands. Her parents lived there the rest of their lives.

On November 29, 1929, when Jennie was 16 years old, she married Joseph D. Cordova. Joseph was a widower and had two little girls from his first marriage. His older daughter was Umatilla and his younger daughter was Alyce. Their mother had died of tuberculosis in 1898 or 1899. Umatilla, a sweet little girl, contracted her mother's disease.

She was placed in an institution for tuberculosis patients and went to be with the Lord while she was there. She was just fourteen years old. When Umatilla died, her father, being single and having to work, couldn't take care of Alyce. So, Alyce went to live with her grandmother and when she was older was placed in a Catholic boarding school.

When Joseph, married Jennie, Alyce was brought home to live with them. At that time, she was nine years old. Over the years, Alyce and Jennie became such good friends that they were like sisters. Jennie and Joseph moved the family from T inidad to Aguilar, Colorado, where Alyce started elementary school.

In the 1930's, when "The Great Depression" started, life became very difficult. Joseph was forced to go wherever he could to find work, while the family stayed in Aguilar. Finally, the whole family was able to move to a farm in Augusta, Colorado. That's when all of the other children were born.

Marian was their first born, then Julie. Next was Priscilla Ruth and David Pete, the first boy. Then Ernestine was born, followed by Sarah Mae, Alex Leroy, Daniel Garfield, Freddie Eleazar, Joseph Del, Jr., Evelyn Esther, Richard Andrew, Eva Mae, Edna Genevieve, Robert Steven (who died at birth), and the baby, Betsy Louise. There were seven boys and nine girls in all, fifteen living children.

Soon after their first child, Marian, was born, God called Joseph into the ministry. He began going from place to place preaching about Yeshua (Jesus) and taking care of several small congregations. Sometimes his older daughters went with him. They brought their instruments and would provide the music in the services.

Jennie never worked outside of the home. She enjoyed being home with her family. She loved her family and her church. She was a happy person who could always find the time to teach her children about God. She enjoyed reading and teaching Biblical truths and songs. She even taught the children some Ladino/Spanish songs. Jennie had a beautiful soprano voice and often sang the old favorite hymns at church. Most of her children began to sing and play musical instruments at a very early age.

She believed in teaching her children how to work. She was always fair, believing that each child should work according to his or her ability. When living on the farm, each person had their own duties. Many interesting things happened on the farm that we all laughed about later, but they seemed very serious at the time.

One example was when David, who was about six years old, was sitting on top of the wooden fence that went around the corral watching the horses. He slipped, fell and broke his arm. At first he laughed because he had been acting like the other big, tough cowboys that either worked on or visited the farm. But, when he realized how serious it was, he burst into tears. Fortunately, he recovered quickly; and, after awhile, he went back to sitting on top of the fence.

Another example was when Daddy and Mama went out shopping in another town one day. The people there thought Mama was Daddy's daughter, which embarrassed Daddy. However, Mama was twenty years younger than Daddy. (He never did show his age).

Jennie worked hard and never complained. She did lots of laundry, cooking, sewing, mending, housework, garden work and canning. Early every morning, she had to get the milk and cream ready for the dairyman's arrival. Some days, she and the children would make butter and cheese. Other days she baked biscuits and pastries, and, once a week, would bake twenty loaves of bread for Saturday and Sunday visitors. She was an extraordinary woman, full of energy and love. Everything she did was done well.

After her husband (my father) died in 1968 and the children were grown, Jennie moved to Indiana where many of the family lived. She lived there for several years, and then went back to Colorado. She is still just as bright and cheerful as ever to those around her. In 2011, she celebrated her 97th birthday, surrounded by her family and friends.

Mama, 1978, Fort Wayne, Indiana

Mama's daddy, "My grandfather," Peter Woodson /Apodaca

CELEBRATION OF LIFE

"Precious in the sight of the Lord is the death of his saints."
(Psalm 116: 15)

Names of my beloved family members who have passed away:

Daddy—Joseph Delfin Cordova—August 31, 1892—September 2, 1968

Half-Sister—Alyce Martinez/Martinez—November 23, 1920—June 16, 1991, First Husband—Max Martinez, Second Husband—Benjamin Martinez—April 25, 1925—February 13, 2006.

Brother—David Pete Cordova, June 21, 1936—October 23, 1962

Sister—Ernestine (Cordova) Ingram, March 31, 1938—June 23, 1974

Sister—Sarah Mae (Cordova) Yoder, August 29, 1939—July 18, 2006

Brother—Alex Leroy Cordova, March 20, 1942—September 2, 1968

Brother—Fred Eleazar Cordova, March 19, 1945—June 23, 1996

Brother—Robert Stephen Cordova, October 15, 1957—October 16, 1957.

Brother-in-Law—Jack Glenn Parton, September 16, 1935—July 12, 2002

"We are confident, I say, and willing rather to be absent from the body, and to be present with the Lord." (II Corinthians 5: 8) KJV

They are in His presence. We are separated for a short time only. As believers in the LORD, we know where they are.

We will meet once again, "In that great reunion day." What a great hope we have!

Julie C. Marlow, September 25, 2009

MY MUSICAL HERITAGE

From the 1860 Census of the Territory of Colorado, which was the earliest family record that I could find, I learned that my great grandfather and grandfather both played the violin.

Apparently, this talent has been passed down through the generations, because my father and his only brother, Ross, also played the violin. Daddy even made one from scratch. I can remember watching him make it. It was a beautiful instrument. (See picture.) He also made a banjo and guitar without a "How-To-Kit" or help from others.

Some of our family's preferred instruments were piano, trumpet; saxophone, flute, clarinet, accordion, drums, guitar, organ, tambourine, cymbals and base guitar, and they still are today. The violin has been the favorite instrument in every generation.

Most of us also sang, for the purposes of thanksgiving, praising, witnessing, teaching and proclaiming the Glory of God in response to His Holy Word.

"Praise him with the sound of the trumpet: praise him with the psaltery and harp.

Praise him with the timbrel and dance: praise him with stringed instruments and organs.

Praise him upon the loud cymbals: praise him upon the high sounding cymbals.

Let everything that hath breath praise the Lord. Praise ye the Lord."

(Psalm 150: 3-5) KJV

At family reunions over the years, it has been wonderful to hear someone sing the old 15th century Judeo (Ladino) songs of praise. They are usually played in minor keys and chords. We all looked forward to family gatherings because it was like an orchestra coming together. Each person would arrive with his or her favorite instrument. Of course, each instrument had to be tuned up and outsiders might consider those sounds noise.

My family enjoyed the sounds, because we eagerly anticipated the beautiful music that would follow, with a great stroke of the beginning note, it seemed that you could forget all your worries and be in God's presence to worship Him.

The music and lyrics were often written by my sister, Marian, and my nephew, Stan. They usually wrote about Adoni (God), Yeshua (Jesus) the Messiah, or Bible story characters like David, Ruth, Daniel and Esther. Other popular scripture songs were from Psalms, Proverbs, and other Bible Books. My brother, Fred, majored in music and was a Band Director at school. Some of my siblings were his students. Because he was a professional and loved music so much, we elected him to be our family music teacher. Everyone seemed to be singing, whistling or humming all the time.

Members of every generation have been able to play an instrument, sing or do both. We are truly a blessed musical family!

"But ye are a chosen generation, a royal priesthood, an holy nation, a peculiar people; that ye should show forth the praises of him who hath called you out of darkness into his marvelous light:" (I Peter 2:9) KJV

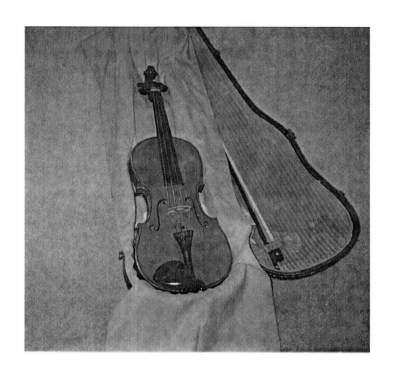

Photo of Daddy's Violin

MY MUSICAL HERITAGE—

SONGS

"SHOUT FOR JOY TO THE LORD" (Psalm 100) and
"LET THE WORD OF CHRIST," (Colossians 3:16,17)
By Stanley Floyd Martinez

"Shout For Joy to the Lord" Page 1

"Shout for Joy to the Lord." Page 2

"Let the Word of Christ"

The music was written by my nephew, Stanley "Stan" Floyd Martinez, son of Alyce (Cordova) and Ben Martinez. He is a Vietnam veteran and has earned the following military awards and medals:

Vietnam Service Medal

Vietnam Campaign Medal

National Defense Medal

Purple Heart Medal (2)

Air Medal (2)

Army Commendation Medal (2)

Bronze Star with "V" for Valor (2)

Combat Infantry Badge and Cross of Gallantry w/palm

Qualified "Expert" (Badge) using the M-14 Rifle, M-60 Machine Gun and Colt 45 Pistol

Qualified "Sharp Shooter" (Badge) for the M-16 Rifle

Awarded two Presidential Unit Citations

Stan enjoys writing poetry and Christian music. He teaches Bible studies, likes to travel and will soon have his own book to share with us. We love and appreciate him for his contributions to the family's musical heritage. At the time of this publication, Stan lives in Maryland.

NAMES, NAMES
AND MORE NAMES

How the children in my family were named has always been very interesting to me. Male and female children alike were often given Biblical names. Sometimes a baby was named to honor a deceased family member or friend. My parents felt this was a way to keep the deceased person's name alive for another generation.

Mama always used a midwife when it was time for a baby to be born. We youngsters would watch with great excitement when the midwife arrived with her black bag. We believed the baby was "in the bag." Sure enough, when the midwife left, we would rush into Mama's room and there would be the baby. It was some years later before we were told that the baby was not "in the bag."

Each baby was dedicated to the Lord in a special ceremony and sometimes a family member, church member or close friend was given the honor of being a witness to the formal naming. In such case, that person had the privilege of adding a middle name or even changing the baby's first name. Mama's and Daddy's approval of the name change had to be obtained ahead of time.

In our family, the children's names are: Miriam, called "Marian;" Julia, called "Julie;" Priscilla Ruth, called "Ruthie;" David Pete, called "Sonny;" Ernestine, called "Ernie;" Sarah Mae, called "Sarah;" Alex Leroy, called "Leroy;" Daniel Garfield, called "Dan;" Freddie Eleazar, called "Freddie;" Joseph Del, Jr., called "Del;" Evelyn Esther, called "Evelyn;" Richard

Andrew, called "Richard;" Eva Mae, called "Eva;" Robert Steven, called "Baby;" Edna Genevieve, called "Edna;" and Betsy Louise, called "Betsy."

Marian, Freddie, Dan and Richard were named by church friends; Julie was named after her paternal grandmother; David Pete was named after his maternal grandfather; Priscilla Ruth, Robert Steven, Ernestine and Alex Leroy were named by family members (Robert died at birth); Eva Mae and Edna Genevieve were named after a family member; and Sarah Mae, Joseph Del, Jr., Evelyn Esther and Betsy Louise were named by our parents.

Some of us acquired a nickname, which was often based upon a physical characteristic, such as petite, pretty eyes or hair color. Richard was sometimes called "Red," Sarah's nickname referred to her petite size and Ernestine's had beautiful eyes. Interestingly, both Sarah and Ernestine were born with one or two teeth already in place.

Because Mama and Daddy had so many children, they were often asked how in the world they could think of enough baby names. They usually answered with "We had a lot of help."

*"Lo, children **are** an heritage of the Lord: **and** the fruit of the womb **is** his reward." (Psalm 127: 3) KJV*

CIRCLE OF LOVE

Memories of Family Meals

"O gives thanks unto the Lord; for he is good: for his mercy endureth forever." "Who giveth food to all flesh: for his mercy endureth forever (Psalm 136:1, 25) KJV

When we were growing up, mealtimes were happy times at our house. As the family gathered at the table, each child moved to his or her usual place. Next, Daddy gave thanks and blessed the meal. Once seated, the children took turns sharing a Bible verse they had memorized. We had to memorize a new Bible verse for each meal.

The smaller children used smaller plates and didn't advance to larger plates until reaching six to eight years of age. If any guests were present, they would be served first. If no guests were present, the children were served first. Then the food was passed around to the rest of the family. Each person would take what he or she wanted or pass it on. When every bowl had been passed, it would then be set in the center of the table.

Daddy and Mama would remind the children of the importance of good manners. If only the family was present, this was usually the time for humor. One of the children would begin to act out by eating in an inappropriate way. This always brought lots of laughter and it helped us to remember the lesson longer.

Our beverage choices included lemonade, cocoa, milk, kool-aid, coffee and tea. We did not have carbonated beverage drinks until later in life. The children were not allowed to drink coffee. It was considered an adult beverage.

Meals consisted of a meat (usually venison, elk, lamb and chicken, sometimes beef or fish), some type of potatoes, gravy and bread or biscuits. Homegrown vegetables were added. They included onions, squash, beans, tomatoes and whatever else was in season. Dessert was usually fruit from the orchard: apples of different varieties, pears, elderberries, cherries and pies made from dried fruit. Cakes and pastries, such as fried apple pies, meat pies and mincemeat pies were reserved for holidays. Some of the holidays we celebrated were Easter, Passover, Hanukkah, Thanksgiving and Christmas.

Between meals, jams, jellies, and peanut butter, on a biscuit were available for snacks. They were kept wrapped up in a dish towel, in a special drawer in the cabinet, and were always available. Mama also preserved or dried fruit for winter use.

When the meal was over and the dishes were removed from the table, Daddy would give the children a current topic or religious belief to debate. Only the children could participate. We were instructed to defend our beliefs and Daddy listened carefully to each child.

After several minutes, he would stop the debate and critique our comments. He would either say, "You did a good job," or he would say, "You need to learn more about this topic before you can defend your views." Sometimes he would say, "You would make a good lawyer," or "You would make a good teacher or preacher." We always wanted to hear Daddy say, "You did a good job.

"Train up a child in the way he should go: and when he is old he will not depart from it." (Proverbs 22: 6) KJV

After the debate, the children tackled the big job of washing the dishes. Mama and her best helper, Marian, whom we all appreciated, gave out the assignments after each meal according to a schedule they had made. The children took turns. One would wash and one would dry and put away the dishes. Our family was so large that we always felt like we were washing dishes in a restaurant. We seldom ate at a restaurant, since Daddy would only let us eat at those places where the meat was prepared a certain way (kosher). Kosher means "clean before God."

From time to time we had an ethnic meal, such as Jewish, Native American, Italian, Greek, Hungarian, German or Dutch. When new people joined our community from other countries, the ladies would share recipes. For some strange reason we never had Mexican food. I guess it was because mama didn't know how to fix it. It was not until fast food restaurants opened in the area that we began to eat it. Today, like most people, we do eat some Mexican foods and share recipes.

Childhood meals were "memory makers." Each meal was special as we sat around the table and joined together in a "Circle of Love."

"I CAN ONLY IMAGINE . . . BEING AN ONLY CHILD"

"Marian, Julie, Priscilla, David, Ernestine, Sarah, Leroy, Daniel, Freddie, Del, Evelyn, Richard, Eva Mae, Edna, Betsy," Mama could be heard calling all our names, in the order of our ages, that was her system of knowing who was missing. This always worked.

Oh, yes, that was my family when I was growing up. Another baby named Robert Steven died at birth, so that left fifteen living children, plus mama and daddy.

On Sunday morning mama would say, "Time for church . . . Let's go!" One of the children would yell, "Oh, Mama! Sarah just pulled off her shoes." "Priscilla, leave your hair bow alone. It will fall off, if you keep touching it." All the older girls had a job to help mama get the family ready for church.

Mama would say, "Has anyone combed Eva Mae's hair yet? Boys are you ready?" One of the boys would yell, "Oh! I can't find my white socks!"

Voices could be heard all over the house as everyone tried to get ready. On and on it went until every one of us was ready and we were on our way to church.

Every Sunday we would go through this all over again. Getting so many children dressed and out of the house was a chore, especially for the older children who were the helpers. Amazingly, once we got to church we had all calmed down and were happy. Those memories are still vivid in my mind and now they are good memories. It was wonderful being part of such a unique, loving and energetic family. I can only imagine . . . being an only child.

Daddy was from the old school of thinking. He considered his children a potential work force. We were his personal army and he was our General. He laid down the law and we were expected to obey immediately and to respect his every word. It took structure and discipline to keep his army going. Daddy could always handle us, but occasionally Mama also had to put her foot down.

All of us children were best friends. There was always the comfort of a sister to soothe hurt feelings and to share our problems with and there were always brothers who loved to tease. Many nights my sister, Marian, would tell us mystery or ghost stories. To create more suspense, she would strum on the guitar for dramatic sound effects. How scared we would get! The entire bunch of us, even the younger boys, would become so frightened that before we could go to sleep, we had to look under the beds and in every closet to see if a "monster" might be hiding there.

I can also remember seeing my little brother, David, doing chores with his tiny pet lamb by his side. It was the sweetest scene you could imagine.

Sometimes we would sing hymns and songs from church and sometimes we sang silly songs that kept us in stitches. When it was time for piano practice, I would say to whoever was at the piano, "It's my turn to practice now. You just finished your turn. Do you have to play the piano all the time?" For some reason I was sometimes left out.

This is another reason why I can't imagine being an only child and not having to share the piano. The house rang with our voices, both day and night, until it was bedtime and everyone was finally asleep.

We made many adjustments and sacrifices as a family and sometimes it didn't seem fair. One time I remember being upset because I didn't have all the material things our friends had. Another was not being able to take vacations and trips to far away countries or even to states around us. This was frustrating to me because I had always wanted to travel. But, all I could do was to read about the faraway places, which I have to admit was fun.

There were only four of my older sisters who were close to my age, so, naturally, we spent more time together. Because of Daddy's strict rules, none of the girls dated until after we left home. However, we were allowed to invite a girl friend to church, a ballgame or a picnic; but my sisters always managed to be first to invite our friends. I was very shy, so that often left me with no one to invite.

My sisters sometimes borrowed my coats, hats, shoes or anything else that they wanted to wear. I didn't feel like I really owned anything. However, I have to admit that I borrowed their things too. When I think about it now, there was no harm done.

"London Bridges Coming Down," "Hide-and-Seek," "Red Rover-Red Rover," jump rope, checkers, playing with paper dolls and working on puzzles were some of the fun games we played. We made our own paper dolls and clothed them with pictures from the Sears catalog. We also played baseball with neighborhood children, mostly at the school ball ground because it was centrally located. When all of the children in my family played, there were enough of us to make up an entire team. Many times we won simply because we stuck together.

One of my fondest memories was of our pillow fights. We had separate bedrooms for the boys and girls. When the boys upset the girls, we took our pillows to the boys' bedroom and started a pillow fight until Mama would stop us. "Girls," she would yell, "Stop that!" Usually it was the girls who started it, since the boys were much younger.

One thing I can remember that always embarrassed me was when people asked how many brothers and sisters I had. I would tell them I was one of nine girls and six boys and they would start laughing. That would make me wish it was different, but I wasn't willing to give up any one of my brothers and sisters. Now that I'm older, I appreciate being from a large family. When we have a reunion today, it's always so much fun.

We're a very musical family, and, when we get together, each person plays his or her favorite instrument and we have a small orchestra. We have a great time playing together and there is always good food, fun and fellowship. I wouldn't have it any other way or change it if I could.

I also have many interesting childhood memories of the time when we lived on a farm. There were lots of chores, so we worked hard and learned many new things, including how to cook and sew. I remember sewing a dress and then having to undo it all simply because I had disobeyed the rules and sewed it on Sunday. We were not allowed to work on Sunday and I had been told many times, "If you sew on Sunday, you will have to take out every stitch with your nose!" Well, that is exactly what I had to do. I had to take out every stitch, but, thankfully, not with my nose. I can still remember that incident, so, needless to say, I have never sewed again on Sunday.

Today, I can only imagine what my life would have been like . . . if I had been an only child.

Note: This article was written for a Writers Club assignment.

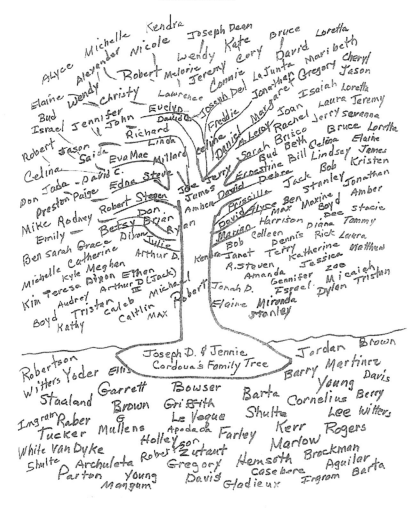

Drawing of the family tree

File:COA Córdoba, Spain.svg

- File
- File history
- File links

COA_Córdoba,_Spain.svg (SVG file, nominally 550 × 963 pixels, file size: 1.63 MB)

This image rendered as PNG in other sizes: 200px, 500px, 1000px, 2000px.

Summary

The "CORDOBA COAT OF ARMS"

CHAPTER 4

MYSTERY OF THE CODED SURNAMES

Shocking Discovery of Coded Surnames

Purpose of Coded Surnames

CHAPTER 4

MYSTERY OF THE
CODED SURNAMES

The oral history passed down in my family was that my ancestors may have been Sephardim (also known as Spanish-Portuguese Jews) who originally came from Israel to Spain. They were also Jews who believed that Yeshua, (Jesus) the Christ (the anointed one), was the Jewish Messiah. That set them apart from traditional Jews as well as from the Catholic Church, the dominant religion in Spain at the time.

As a result, they felt that it would be wise to keep their Messianic Jewish beliefs a secret. That way, they could assimilate into the community without fear of persecution. They needed to devise a system whereby they could identify each other, but not be identified by non-Messianic believers.

I want to share with you what I learned through my personal research about how the system might have worked.

First of all, I learned that there are those today who have never heard that the area encompassing Spain and Portugal was once named "Sefarad." That fact is recorded in the Bible in Obadiah 20 and other places.

It was in the 1400's that Queen Isabella and King Ferdinand, hoping to unite Spain and bring their two kingdoms together, required everyone in the country to convert to Catholicism (Christianity) or be turned over to the Spanish Inquisition to be tortured or killed. Many Jews converted in name only, but continued to observe their special Jewish feasts and customs in secret. When discovered, Catholics called the Jews "New Christians" or "*Marranos,*" *(pigs).* This was a crude insult referring to the fact that Jews don't eat pork.

An estimated number of Jews, possibly more than 200,000, fled Spain by August 2, 1492. They scattered throughout the world. Wherever they settled, they still lived in fear of being discovered and turned over to the feared Spanish Inquisition. It is my belief that my ancestors eventually settled in New Mexico and Colorado. They brought with them the secret code names they had developed earlier.

The Origin of Coded Surnames

The secret code names were actually family names (surnames or last names) that were already in use, but that specifically referred to a shrub, tree, something else in nature, or a city. That way they could recognize each another when names were exchanged and would know immediately those they shared a similar faith and background. If a person's last name was not that of a shrub, tree, something else in nature, or a city, it was very likely that the person was not a Sephardic Messianic Jew.

There were a few exceptions. For example, names ending in "ez" or "za" referred in Spanish or Ladino (Judaeo-Spanish) to "erez," meaning "You are from Israel." Some family names ending in "ez" or "za" are Gomez, Martinez, Gonzalez, Espinoza, Cortez, Lopez, and Perez, are but a few. Ladino is an ancient language spoken by descendants of the Jewish population expelled from Spain. The language was kept fairly simple and untouched, or pure until years later, because they were so far away and had no direct dealings with the mother country or any other country.

Once my ancestors settled in Colorado and New Mexico, this coding was fairly successful because it allowed the Sephardic Messianic Jews to become an integral part of the community without being identified by anyone other than those of like origin and faith.

However, in the 1800's, when more and more settlers came into the territory from all over the world, some of the newcomers began to suspect that there were Messianic Jews living among them. Mostly, it was because those Jews claimed to be descendants of the early church started by Jesus and his Jewish followers and because they secretly observed special feast days that were not called by their traditional Jewish names. As a result, once again, the persecution began.

They were persecuted by two groups. First, there were the non-Jewish settlers who would not give them a job, allow them to buy a home, pursue an education or worship in their churches. Second, there were the Jews who did not believe that Yeshua, (Jesus Christ), was the Jewish Messiah. For those that knew that Messianic Jews were in the community they made it rather clear that Messianic Jews were not welcome in their synagogues.

Fortunately, over time both the prejudice and persecution diminished to the degree that later generations living in the territory never realized that Sephardic Messianic Jews had ever lived there.

Apparently, not all Messianic Jews experienced persecution because I have distant family members today who don't know, or might not accept if they did know, that they are Sephardic Messianic Jews. However, if they will read this book, they will come face to face with factual proof of their heritage, which includes unique DNA evidence.

I, myself, am very proud to be a direct descendant of the Sephardic Jews. It was their method of communicating through coded family names and loyalty to their Messianic beliefs that, I think, deserve our appreciation and applause.

More about Surnames

I was surprised to learn, through my research, that surnames were not always popular. The Chinese were the first known people to acquire more than one name. About 2852 B.C., the Emperor Fushi is said to have decreed the use of family names.

The Romans also used only one name, but later they began using three names. First was the "*praenomen*," the person's given name. Second was the "*nomen*," this indicated the clan. Last was the "*cognomen*," or family name.

For example, Julius Caesar's full name was Gaius (given name) Julius (clan name) Caesar (family name). Family names became so long that about the time of the fall of the Roman Empire single names once again came into use. It was the Christian Crusaders that spread the use of family names throughout Western Europe.

In order to have continuity in a family, names were passed down from one generation to another. For example, parents might name a child after a parent, grandparent or great grandparent.

To avoid confusion when two people had the same given name and lived in the same community, additional information was added. For example, if parents named their son Peter and there was another person named Peter living up the hill from them, that person would become known as Peter Hill. In the Hebrew/Spanish Ladino dialect, he would be called Peter de Monte (Peter from the Hill). A man by the name of David, living in the City of Aguilar, would become David de Aguilar or David Aguilar.

In my family, there is a tradition of giving a child the name of a grandparent. Now several generations have someone in it with the same given name, either Hebrew or Christian. For example, I was named Julia after my paternal grandmother.

When I began researching my own maiden name, *Cordova (Cordoba)*, I learned that it was the name of a City in Spain, making it a coded surname. It was also spelled Cordero, meaning "sheepherder." This was a little puzzling to me because, outside of my own family, I have been unable to find anyone with the coded surnames of Cordova, Cordoba or Cordero. It's quite possible that my family has distant relatives that we have never met and lost track of when my father was orphaned as a young child.

In most countries, non-Sephardic Jewish family names were the last to be developed. In Europe, Jews usually lived apart from others in a secluded community so they probably didn't feel the need for family names. However, laws passed in Europe in the early 1800's compelled them to adopt family names. Many of them chose combinations of various Jewish words, such as gold, silver, rose, mountain and valley, (In Hebrew:

"rosen", "berg" and "thal"). They formed family names such as Goldberg, Silverstein and Rosenthal. Some adopted the name of the city where they were born, such as London or Modena.

Others created family names with religious connotations. Katz is an abbreviation of "Kohen Tzedek," the Hebrew name for "Priest of Righteousness." Still others used given names for family names, such as Benjamin and Levy. Many of these names are still in use today.

For anyone with an interest in genealogy, a study of their family name can be a fascinating project. They will be surprised to learn that each family has a unique DNA that can be traced all the way back to its country of origin.

CHAPTER 5

LADINO,
THE LOST DIALECT

The Big Secret of Southeastern Colorado
Ancient 15th Century Judaeo/Spanish Dialect
Spoken by First Settlers of Colorado
Sample of Ladino Dialect (Spanish: Judaeo)

CHAPTER 5

LADINO, THE LOST DIALECT

THE BIG SECRET

OF SOUTHEASTERN COLORADO

Historians have only recently discovered and expressed much interest in a lost dialect spoken by the early pioneers of Southeastern Colorado and Northern New Mexico. This dialect was a 15th century Judaeo-Spanish language called "Ladino" that was spoken by their Sephardic (Sefarad in Hebrew) Jewish ancestors who were expelled from Spain and Portugal from 1492 through the 1500's. In an effort to escape the Spanish Inquisition of Torquemada that persecuted non-Catholics, their ancestors began scattering throughout the world in the same year that Christopher Columbus set out to explore what we now call "The Americas." It is quite possible that this was the language spoken by Christopher Columbus and his crew of sailors.

The Sephardic Jews brought their language with them to the New World and continued to speak Ladino without realizing that it was a very unique and ancient dialect. It was the only language they knew and spoke. The dialect continued to be passed down from one generation to the next. As people from other cultures joined their community, the newcomers assumed this dialect was simply the ordinary local Spanish dialect, not realizing it was the ancient, now obsolete Ladino, that these people had spoken in Spain and brought with them.

Because of the influx of other cultures, it was inevitable that each new generation of Sephardic Jews would begin to learn new languages. Less and less Ladino was spoken and it began to lose words and phrases, showing clear signs of dying off. When a person couldn't remember the original words, other phrases were adopted and substituted.

At one point, at least eighty-eight different languages were spoken in Colorado. In the late 1800's and early 1900's, Southeastern Colorado began to develop into a coal mining area, which brought about a growing population and even more new languages.

Unfortunately, subsequent generations didn't comprehend the importance of preserving the dialect. Only the older people who remained in the area continued to speak Ladino in its unadulterated form. Most families made no effort to preserve it. The only written examples of the pure dialect were those saved in the records and notes of family Bibles.

Until my generation, this ancient 15th century dialect of Ladino was spoken in my own family. When I took Spanish in High School, I realized that the Spanish taught in Spanish Class was not what I had learned from my family. That was the first clue that something was different.

When I began the research for this book, older Ladino speaking people were very helpful to me. Some elderly members of my family and other families had memorized entire chapters of scriptures from the 15th century Ladino or Castilian Spanish Bible, which they must have brought with them from Spain

It was an amazing experience to listen to those who had not forgotten the ancient dialect. It is unbelievable that many families today are still reluctant to share historical information or to leave any written records. They believe they are still trying to escape the long arm of the Spanish Inquisition, because they are Messianic Jews.

Ladino differs from modern Spanish in that it is Old Spanish that includes forms and words that are now obsolete, much like the Old English language, example the (King James) version of the Bible.

It is a vernacular and literary language that is spoken by most of the Sephardic Jews scattered throughout the Mediterranean area and other countries. In the Eastern Mediterranean area it is estimated that at least 200,000 Jews still speak Ladino, including those who now live in Israel.

As mentioned earlier, it was only recently that historians discovered this ancient dialect is still spoken in Southeastern Colorado and have begun to show an interest in it.

"Like Yiddish of the Romance languages," Ladino incorporates Spanish words and Hebrew words into an archaic Spanish syntax and vocabulary. It is written in Hebrew characters, except by those who have adopted more modern Spanish. It has evolved into a cultural assimilation due to the increasing availability of contemporary Spanish printed matter.

However, it still possesses a great literary heritage. It was the secrecy surrounding the dialect that prompted me to write this book in order to explain why the Ladino dialect has remained so protected and hidden. It would be a tragic loss for this rich and beautiful dialect to be lost in the annals of history.

My hope is to preserve its memory. I believe that its legacy is far-reaching. It seems to me that this dialect was divinely spared and saved by providence.

Otherwise, the evidence of this unique and sacred language would have been totally lost without anyone ever knowing of its existence.

SAMPLE OF LADINO DIALECT

SPANISH: JUDAEO

HEBREW CHARACTER

פרינסיפּיין דיל איבֿאנגֿיליין די יׂשׂוׂע איל מׂשׂיח, ¹איׂזׂו :
דיל דייו; קומו איסמׂה איסקריטו אין לוס פרופֿיטׂאס:

2 ²היק, יו אינבֿיאו מי מינסאֿזֿירו דילֿאנטֿי די טוס פֿאסים,

3 קי אטֿאררנֿזֿארה טו קאמינו דילֿאנטֿי די טי. ³טֿח די פרינומירו
אין איל דיזׂיירטו: אטֿאריזֿאד איל קאמינו דיל סינֿייוגֿ, אינ-

4 דיריסׂאֿד סוס סינדירום. איסטֿאבֿֿה יוחנן בׂאפֿטֿיחֿאהׂדו אין
איל דיזׂיירטו, אי פרידיקֿאנֿדו איל בׂאפֿטֿיחֿמו די אריסׂינֿטֿי-

5 מייניטו טֿאֿרֿה סירדֿון די פׂוקֿאֿדׂום. אי סֿאלׂיׂהׂה אה איל

Mk 1. 1-4   1922

Judaeo-Spanish, or Ladino, is spoken by descendants of the Jewish population expelled from Spain under Torquemada in 1492. The more than 100,000 Ladino-speaking Sephardic Jews are mostly settled in urban areas in the eastern Mediterranean area, and at least 20,000 Ladino immigrants now live in Israel. 'The Yiddish of the Romance languages', Ladino incorporates modern loan words and Hebraisms into a basically archaic Spanish syntax and vocabulary, which is essentially 15th-century Spanish. Like Yiddish, Judaeo-Spanish possesses a great literary heritage. It is written in Hebrew character, except by those who have adopted more modern Spanish usage, owing to cultural assimilation and the increased availability of contemporary Spanish printed matter.

CHAPTER 6

BELIEFS AND THE JEWISH ROOTS OF OUR FAITH

MY SEPHARDIC MESSIANIC JEWISH FAMILY

My Introduction to the Ten Commandments

The Ten Commandments

The Origin of the "Missing Link"

Part One: Divine Curses

Part Two: Divine Curses

Divine Blessings

CHAPTER 6

BELIEFS AND THE JEWISH ROOTS OF OUR FAITH

My Sephardic Messianic Jewish Family

In Old Testament times, the Israelites alone believed that there was only One God and that it was He who held all power in His hands. It was He who created the Universe, including mankind. *(Nehemiah 9: 6) KJV.*

"The fool hath said in his heart, There is no God . . ." (Psalms 14:1) KJV

They believed in the great God "I AM,"

"And God said unto Moses, I AM THAT I AM: and he said, Thus shall thou say unto the children of Israel, I AM hath sent me unto you."

(Exodus 3:14) KJV

Through Moses, the great leader, God gave the Torah to the people, which contained His laws and Commandments. The Torah is also called the "Pentateuch" and refers to the first five books of the Hebrew Scriptures. It is an accepted belief that God gave Moses, stone tablets on which God used His finger to carve His statutes for living. The statutes on those tablets were called "The Ten Commandments."

This great God gives a description of Himself in the Book of Genesis, in which He tells us that He is a spirit being, with no beginning or end. He is eternal . . . the Alpha and the Omega.

God formed His creation by speaking the words *"Let there be . . ."* and it immediately came into existence. He spoke the words, *"Let there be light:"* and, at once there was light. All of creation was spoken into being in this manner. *(Genesis 1: 1-31) KJV*

God's creation was made in a very orderly way. He created the seasons, nights, days and years. He provided vegetation and animals as food for man to eat.

By looking at creation, the earth and all that is in it, man should be able to see the handiwork of a creative being that is far more wonderful than what we can imagine. The Bible tells us that,"

And the earth was without form, and void; and darkness was upon the face of the deep. And the Spirit of God moved upon the face of the waters."

(Genesis 1: 2) KJV

According to the Holy Scripture, this information was recorded in the first book of the Bible, named Genesis, (Book of Beginnings).

My family believes that the Bible is the divine, inspired, living Word of God. We believe in both the Old Testament (Old Covenant) and the New Testament (New Covenant). We believe the Bible is the final authority.

"All scripture is given by inspiration of God, and is profitable for doctrine, for reproof, for correction, for instruction in righteousness:" (*II Timothy 3:16*) *KJV*

"Being born again, not of corruptible seed, but of incorruptible, by the word of God, which liveth and abideth for ever. For all flesh is as grass, and all the glory of man as the flower of grass. The grass withereth, and the flower thereof falleth away:

But the word of the Lord endureth for ever. And this is the word which by the gospel is preached unto you."(I Peter 1: 23-25) KJV

We believe in Jehovah (**YHWH,** pronounced Yah-way**, I AM,** or He which is, or He who is truly present; Self-existent *(Exodus 3:14-15) KJV,* **El-Elyon** (Most High God/Exalted One), *(Genesis14:18-20) KJV,* **Adoni,** (Lord Master), *(Psalm 2:4) KJV* and **El Shaddai,** (Almighty God), *(Genesis 17:1-2) KJV.*

These are just some of the names of God.

We believe in Yeshua (Jesus), meaning "Salvation," (Ha Mashiach), meaning the "Anointed One," the only begotten Son of God, who became God Incarnate. He is both fully God and fully man, conceived by the Holy Spirit and born to a Jewish virgin, Miriam (Mary). His birth was prophesied many years before He was born, with explicit details concerning His birth, His family, His life, and His death.

"In this was manifested the love of God toward us, because that God sent his only begotten Son into the world, that we might live through him." (I John 4: 9) KJV

"And in the sixth month the angel Gabriel was sent from God unto a city of Galilee, named Nazareth,

To a virgin espoused to a man whose name was Joseph, of the house of David; and the virgin's name was Mary.

And the angel came in unto her, and said, Hail, thou that art highly favoured, the Lord is with thee: blessed art thou among women.

And when she saw him, she was troubled at his saying, and cast in her mind what manner of salutation this should be. And the angel said unto her, Fear not, Mary: for thou hast found favour with God. And, behold, thou shalt conceived in thy womb, and bring forth a son, and shalt call his name (Yeshua) JESUS.

He shall be great, and shall be called the Son of the Highest: and the Lord God shall give unto him the throne of his father David:

And he shall reign over the house of Jacob for ever; and of his kingdom there shall be no end.

Then said Mary unto the angel, how shall this be, seeing I know not a man?

And the angel answered and said unto her, The Holy Ghost shall come upon thee, and the power of the Highest shall overshadow thee: therefore also that holy thing which shall be born of thee shall be called the Son of God.

And, behold, thy cousin Elisabeth, she hath also conceived a son in her old age: and this is the sixth month with her, who was called barren. For with God nothing shall be impossible." (Luke 1: 26-37) KJV

"Now the birth of Jesus Christ was on this wise: When as his mother Mary was espoused to Joseph, before they came together, she was found with child of the Holy Ghost. Then Joseph her husband, being a just man, and not willing to make her a public example, was minded to put her away privily.

But while he thought on these things, behold, the angel of the Lord appeared unto him in a dream, saying, Joseph, thou son of David, fear not to take unto thee Mary thy wife: for that which is conceived in her is of the Holy Ghost.

And she shall bring forth a son, and thou shalt call his name JESUS: for he shall save his people from their sins." (Matthew 1: 18-21) KJV

My family believes that Yeshua (Jesus), by virtue of His miraculous birth and sinless life, voluntarily gave Himself as the perfect atoning sacrifice for the sins of Israel and all mankind; and, by His death, made it possible for all mankind to be reconciled to God.

"But God commendeth his love toward us, in that, while we were yet sinners, Christ died for us." (Romans 5: 8) KJV

"Grace be to you and peace from God the Father, and from our Lord Jesus Christ, who gave himself for our sins, that he might deliver us from this present evil world, according to the will of God and our Father:

To whom be glory forever and ever. Amen." (Galatians 1:3-5) KJV

"And almost all things are by the law purged with blood; and without shedding of blood is no remission."

"So Christ was once offered to bear the sins of many; and unto them that look for him shall he appear the second time without sin unto salvation."

(Hebrews 9:22, 28) KJV See also (Hebrews 10: 1-39) KJV

New Covenant

"Behold, the days come, saith the Lord, that I will make a new covenant with the house of Israel, and with the house of Judah." (Jeremiah 31: 31) KJV

My family believes that Yeshua (Jesus) died on the cross (the tree), and on the third day He arose from the dead and ascended into Heaven where He is seated at the right hand of God the Father, as our intercessor and advocate, the only mediator between God and man.

We believe that Yeshua (Jesus) will soon return. He will descend from Heaven to gather (Rapture) to Himself the true believers, those who have accepted Yeshua (Jesus) as the Messiah.

"But I would not have you to be ignorant, brethren, concerning them which are asleep, that ye sorrow not, even as others which have no hope.

For if we believe that Jesus died and rose again, even so them also which sleep in Jesus will God bring with him.

For this we say unto you by the word of the Lord, that we which are alive and remain unto the coming of the Lord shall not prevent them which are asleep.

For the Lord himself shall descend from heaven with a shout, with the voice of the archangel, and with the trump of God: and the dead in Christ shall rise first:

Then we which are alive and remain shall be caught up together with them in the clouds, to meet the Lord in the air: and so shall we ever be with the Lord.

Wherefore comfort one another with these words.

(I Thessalonians 4: 13-18) KJV.

We believe all men are sinners by nature. It started with Adam and Eve. We also believe that we are all in need of salvation, which can only be accomplished by repentance and confessing a belief in Yeshua (Jesus as the Messiah). Salvation is made possible by God's grace and the atoning blood of Yeshua (Jesus), His death and resurrection

"For all have sinned, and come short of the glory of God;

Being justified freely by his grace through the redemption that is in Christ Jesus:" (Romans 3: 23-24) KJV

"That if thou shalt confess with thy mouth the Lord Jesus, and shalt believe in thine heart that God hath raised him from the dead, thou shalt be saved.

For with the heart man believeth unto righteousness; and with the mouth confession is made unto salvation."

"For whosoever shall call upon the name of the Lord shall be saved."

(Romans 10: 9-10, 13) KJV

"For by grace are ye saved through faith; and that not of yourselves: it is the gift of God: Not of works, lest any man should boast." (Ephesians 2: 8-9) KJV

As recipients of God's wonderful gift of salvation, we have but to ask the Father for forgiveness of our sins and He will forgive us.

"If we confess our sins, he is faithful and just to forgive us our sins, and to cleanse us from all unrighteousness. (I John 1: 9) KJV

After a person has accepted the gift of salvation, he or she should seek to be "filled with and sealed by" the Holy Spirit, as a separate and distinct experience, in order to be endued with power for the Lord's service (work) *"And [Jesus], being assembled together with them [his disciples], commanded them that they should not depart from Jerusalem, but wait for the promise of the Father, which, saith he, ye have heard of me.*

For John [John the Baptist] truly baptized with water; but ye shall be baptized with the Holy Ghost not many days hence."

"But ye shall receive power, after that the Holy Ghost is come upon you: and ye shall be witnesses unto me both in Jerusalem, and in all Judaea, and in Samaria, and unto the uttermost part of the earth."

(Acts 1: 4-5, 8) KJV See also *(Acts 2: 1-21, 38-39) KJV*

"If a son shall ask bread of any of you that is a father, will he give him a stone? or if he ask a fish, will he for a fish give him a serpent?

Or if he shall ask an egg, will he offer him a scorpion?

If ye then, being evil, know how to give good gifts unto your children: how much more shall your heavenly Father give the Holy Spirit to them that ask him?" (Luke 11: 11-13) KJV

"In whom ye also trusted [Jesus], after that ye heard the word of truth, the gospel of your salvation: in whom also after that ye believed, ye were sealed with that Holy Spirit of promise, Which is the earnest of our inheritance until the redemption of the purchased possession, unto the praise of his glory." (Ephesians 1: 13-14) KJV

We believe in tithing and love offerings, only for the purpose of supporting the Lord's work. One-tenth is the measure of one's tithe that is required. (*Leviticus 27*) *KJV*

"Bring ye all the tithes into the storehouse, that there may be meat in mine house, and prove me now herewith, saith the Lord of hosts, if I will not open you the windows of heaven, and pour you out a blessing, that there shall not be room enough to receive it.

And I will rebuke the devourer for your sakes, and he shall not destroy the fruits of your ground; neither shall your vine cast her fruit before the time in the field, saith the Lord of hosts." (Malachi 3: 10-11) KJV

Give, and it shall be given unto you; good measure, pressed down, and shaken together, and running over, shall men give into your bosom. For with the same measure that ye mete withal it shall be measured to you again."

(Luke 6: 38) KJV

Heaven and Hell

We believe in a literal Heaven and Hell.

"And I John [the apostle] saw the holy city, New Jerusalem, coming down from God out of heaven, prepared as a bride adorned for her husband.

And I heard a great voice out of heaven saying, Behold, the tabernacle of God is with men, and he will dwell with them, and they shall be his people, and God himself shall be with them, and be their God.

And God shall wipe away all tears from their eyes; and there shall be no more death, neither sorrow, nor crying, neither shall there be any more pain: for the former things are passed away." (Revelation 21: 2-4) KJV

"After this manner therefore pray ye: Our Father which art in heaven, Hallowed be thy name. Thy kingdom come. Thy will be done in earth, as it is in heaven." (Matthew 6: 9-10) KJV

God shall come to judge the living and the dead and His Kingdom (New Jerusalem) shall have no end.

"And there was given him [Jesus] dominion, and glory, and a kingdom, that all people, nations, and languages, should serve him: his dominion is an everlasting dominion, which shall not pass away, and his kingdom that which shall not be destroyed." (Daniel 7:14) KJV

"When the Son of man shall come in his glory, and all the holy angels with him, then shall he sit upon the throne of his glory:

And before him shall be gathered all nations: and he shall separate them one from another, as a shepherd divideth his sheep from the goats:

And he shall set the sheep on his right hand, but the goats on the left

Then shall the King say unto them on his right hand, Come, ye blessed of my Father, inherit the kingdom prepared for you from the foundation of the world:"

"Then shall he say also unto them on the left hand, Depart from me, ye cursed, into everlasting fire, prepared for the devil and his angels:"

(Matthew 25: 31-34, 41) KJV

We also believe in the following observances:

<u>Water Baptism by Immersion</u>

Jesus is our example when He Himself was baptized.

"And it came to pass in those days, that Jesus came from Nazareth of Galilee, and was baptized of John [the Baptist] in Jordan.

And straightway coming up out of the water, he saw the heavens opened, and the Spirit like a dove descending upon him:"

(Mark 1: 9-10) KJV

"Then cometh Jesus from Galilee to Jordan unto John [the Baptist], to be baptized of him. But John forbad him, saying, I have need to be baptized of thee, and comest thou to me?

And Jesus answering said unto him, Suffer it to be so now: for thus it becometh us to fufil all righteousness. Then he suffered him.

And Jesus, when he was baptized, went up straightway out of the water: and, lo, the heavens were opened unto him, and he saw the Spirit of God descending like a dove, and lighting upon him:

And lo a voice from heaven, saying, this is my beloved Son, in whom I am well pleased."

(Matthew 3: 13-17) KJV

"And Jesus came and spake unto them [disciples], saying, All power is given unto me in heaven and in earth

Go ye therefore, and teach all nations, baptizing them in the name of the Father, and of the Son, and of the Holy Ghost:

Teaching them to observe all things whatsoever I have commanded you: and, lo, I am with you always, even unto the end of the world. Amen." *(Matthew 28: 18-20) KJV*

Passover

In the Old Testament (Old Covenant) Passover was observed to commemorate when God miraculously freed his people, the Israelites, from Egyptian slavery. He sent Ten plagues, or punishments, on the Egyptians. The last plague or punishment was when God slayed all the firstborn in the land of Egypt, but passed over the Jewish homes of those who obeyed His command to place the blood of a sacrificial lamb upon the lintel and two side posts of the door.

"And they shall take of the blood, and strike it on the two side posts and on the upper door post of the houses, wherein they shall eat it."

And verse 22:

"And ye shall take a bunch of hyssop, and dip it in the blood that is in the basin, and strike the lintel and the two side posts with the blood that is in the basin; and none of you shall go out at the door of his house until the morning" *(Exodus 12:7 and 22) KJV*

I suddenly realized when I read this about having a bunch of hyssop dipped in the blood that was in the basin, and, by striking the top of the door going down, across the two sides posts, it would look like a cross made with the blood of the lamb. How amazing!

Then I could truly see that the blood of the lamb, Yeshua (Jesus Christ, the Messiah, The Anointed One) has become, by His death on the cross and shedding of His blood, the Passover Lamb, the perfect sacrifice. He made this sacrifice once, for all mankind, not to cover their sins for one year, but forever!

"And it came to pass, that at midnight the Lord smote all the firstborn in the land of Egypt, from the firstborn of Pharaoh that sat on his throne unto the firstborn of the captive that was in the dungeon; and all the firstborn of cattle

And Pharaoh rose up in the night, he, and all his servants, and all the Egyptians; and there was a great cry in Egypt; for there was not a house where there was not one dead." (Exodus 12: 29-30) KJV

"And it shall come to pass, when your children shall say unto you, What mean ye by this service?

That ye shall say, it is the sacrifice of the Lord's Passover, who passed over the houses of the children of Israel in Egypt, when he smote the Egyptians, and delivered our houses. And the people bowed the head and worshipped." (Exodus 12: 26-27) KJV

Long ago in Israel, every Jewish man had to go once a year and offer a sacrifice for the sins of his household. He would bring a lamb a year old, without blemish, and offer it to God. He would slay the lamb, shed blood, and this sacrifice was a covering for sin and good for one year; it had to be repeated every year.

But, when Jesus came and died on the cross, He became the lamb that was sacrificed once and for all, to not only to cover the sins of mankind but to wipe them out forever. Today, because of this, man does not have to kill an innocent lamb so that his sins can be forgiven for one year. Jesus has already done it, not for a year but forever!

<u>Communion: The Lord's Supper</u>

When the Lord celebrated His last Seder (Passover Dinner) with His disciples, it was at that time that He instituted the Lord's Supper (Communion), as a perpetual memorial, fulfilling the meaning of Passover. He used the traditional elements of broken Matzah and the third cup of wine (Cup of Redemption), to point to Himself as the sacrificial lamb that was to die for our sins. We are mindful of the profound meaning our Lord gave it, and are grateful for all of His good gifts.

"And as they [the disciples] did eat, Jesus took bread, and blessed, and broke it, and gave to them, and said, Take, eat: this is my body.

And he took the cup, and when he had given thanks, he gave it to them: and they all drank of it.

And he said unto them, This is my blood of the New Testament, which is shed for many.

Verily I say unto you, I will drink no more of the fruit of the vine, until that day that I drink it new in the kingdom of God." (Mark 14: 22-25) KJV

During the Old Testament observance of the Passover meal, the third cup (Cup of Redemption) represented the promise of a New Covenant with the house of Israel.

"Behold, the days come, saith the Lord, that I will make a new covenant with the house of Israel, and with the house of Judah:

Not according to the covenant that I made with their fathers in the day that I took them by the hand to bring them out of the land of Egypt; which my covenant they brake, although I was an husband unto them, saith the Lord:

But this shall be the covenant that I will make with the house of Israel; ***After those days, saith the Lord, I will put my law in their inward parts, and write it in their hearts; and will be their God, and they shall be my people:" (Jeremiah 31: 31-33) KJV***

Dedication of Babies

My family dedicates our children when they are babies. Later, at the age of accountability, we baptize them. A Rabbi or Pastor presides.

"And they [parents] brought young children to him [Jesus], that he should touch them: and his disciples rebuked those that brought them.

But when Jesus saw it, he was much displeased, and said unto them, Suffer the little children to come unto me, and forbid them not: for of such is the kingdom of God. Verily I say unto you, Whosoever shall not receive the kingdom of God as a little child, he shall not enter therein." (Mark 10: 13-15) KJV

The Marriage Ceremony

We believe that marriage is a union of one man and one woman. *"And he [Jesus] answered and said unto them [Pharisees and others], Have ye not read, that he which made them at the beginning made them male and female, And said, For this cause shall a man leave father and mother, and shall cleave to his wife: and they twain shall be one flesh?*

Wherefore they are no more twain, but one flesh. What therefore God hath joined together, let not man put asunder." (Matthew 19: 4-6) KJV.

"For this cause shall a man leave his father and mother, and shall be joined unto his wife, and they two shall be one flesh."

(Ephesians 5: 31) KJV

Anointing with Oil (New Covenant)

This is the prescribed manner for healing the sick. *"Is any sick among you? let him call for the elders of the church; and let them pray over him, anointing him with oil in the name of the Lord: And the prayer of faith shall* save the sick, and the Lord shall raise him up; and if he have committed sins, *they shall be forgiven him."* (James 5: 14-15) KJV

Anointing oil is symbolic of the Holy Spirit and His healing power. Today we can obtain anointing oil through Jewish Resources or Christian bookstores.

<u>Laying on of Hands</u>

This was done by Jesus and His disciples in the first century church. The laying on of hands is used in consecration, ordination, blessing and healing.

"Now when the sun was setting, all they that had any sick with divers diseases brought them unto him [Jesus]; and he laid his hands on every one of them, and healed them." (Luke 4: 40) KJV

Because of my belief in the Holy Scriptures and my study of them, I feel that the Lord has equipped and prepared me, just as He did with Esther in the Bible, ..."for such a time as this"... *(Esther 4:14) KJV* I consider it a privilege to share with, and, possibly, influence both family and friends about the Messiah, His teachings and His desire to redeem all mankind. Jesus is the Passover Lamb, who died on the cross so that we might be forgiven of our sins forever. Now, He lives eternally in our hearts.

I will continue to write and speak, as He guides me, so that I may bring honor to His Holy name.

To God is the Glory!

CHAPTER 6

MY INTRODUCTION TO THE TEN COMMANDMENTS

Early In Life

My introduction to the Ten Commandments came early in life. As a child, I heard my parents talking about God and His commandments. I often wondered why some people didn't want to follow God's teachings. Even as a child, I felt a certain urgency to tell my friends about God.

I wanted them to realize that God loves all human beings because He created us.

The Book of Revelation says:

"You are worthy, our Lord and God, to receive glory and honor and power, for you created all things, and by your will they were created and have their being." (Revelation 4:11) NIV

Each of us needs to know why we were born and what God's purpose is for our life. We are all unique individuals, with no two alike. God has given us different gifts and talents to be used for His glory. Not all men acknowledge it, but God has instilled in each of us a heartfelt desire to love, serve and worship Him. The Book of Psalms give us a beautiful example of a man named King David, whose greatest pleasure in life was to worship God in music, praise and prayer.

"And like unto him was there no king before him, that turned to the Lord with all his heart, and with all his soul, and with all his might, according to all the law of Moses; neither after him arose there any like him." (II Kings 23: 25) KJV

God's Laws: the Ten Commandments

The Ten Commandments and the rest of God's laws are for all people in every generation. If we are to believe in the Holy Scriptures, we must believe them all. We can't pick and choose what we like and what we want to believe.

"This book of the law shall not depart out of thy mouth; but thou shalt meditate therein day and night, that thou mayest observe to do according to all that is written therein: for then thou shalt make thy way prosperous, and then thou shalt have good success."

(Joshua 1: 8) KJV

God knew that man would need rules and regulations to live by, so that there would be order in the world and in our lives. For that reason, He gave us the Bible as a guide for living, which includes the Ten Commandments. Can you imagine what the world would be like if we didn't have God's guidance or any kind of rules? The world would collapse into a state of chaos.

God chose Moses to lead His people out of bondage in Egypt and through the wilderness into the "promised land." This was a very large group of people. I read in a census taken at the time that the group included 603,550 males above the age of twenty. That number did not include the Levites, (Priesthood), women or children. It only took a few days before many of the people became disenchanted and started complaining and rebelling against Moses. It quickly became apparent to Moses that he would need more of God's help; so he cried out to God, who heard his prayer and answered him. God instructed him to bring the people to Mount Sinai.

Immediately, Moses led the people to Mount Sinai. There they witnessed and heard a terrifying thunderstorm, an earthquake, a supernatural trumpet blast and roaring flames at the top of the mountain. God instructed Moses to come up onto the mountain alone, which he did. There God carved the Ten Commandments, with his finger, onto two stone tablets.

Today, all countries have laws and regulations for their people to follow, regardless of where the country is located. Our own country was founded on Judeo-Christian principles. As a result, our laws reveal a striking similarity to God's laws.

"Where there is ignorance of God, the people run wild; but what a wonderful thing it is for a nation to know and keep his laws!

(Proverbs 29: 18) TLB (The Living Bible)

Some people think that because the Ten Commandments are located in the Old Testament (Old Covenant), they only apply to the Jewish people. However, in the New Testament (New Covenant) we learn that Yeshua (Jesus), God's only begotten Son, came to earth not to do away with Old Testament laws, but to **fulfill them** and to offer us a way to obtain eternal life.

(Jesus speaking) "Think not that I am come to destroy the law, or the prophets: I am not come to destroy, but to fulfill. (Matthew 5:17) KJV

"For verily I say unto you, Till heaven and earth pass, one jot or one tittle [dot of the "i" or cross of the "t"] shall in no wise pass from the law, till all be fulfilled.

Whosoever therefore shall break one of these least commandments, and shall teach men so, he shall be called the least in the kingdom of heaven: but whosoever shall do and teach them, the same shall be called great in the kingdom of heaven." (Matthew 5: 18-19) KJV

Idol Worship Forbidden

When I was older, I read in the Old Testament about man creating false gods for himself. It distressed me to realize just how far man had drifted away from the one true God. God's first, second and third commandments forbid the worship of graven images.

"Thou shalt have no other gods before me.

Thou shalt not make unto thee any graven image, or any likeness of anything that is in heaven above, or that is in the earth beneath, or that is in the water under the earth:

Thou shalt not bow down thyself to them, nor serve them: for I the Lord thy God am a jealous God, visiting the iniquity of the fathers upon the children unto the third and fourth generation of them that hate me;

And showing mercy unto thousands of them that love me, and keeps my commandments."

(Exodus 20: 3-6) KJV

Sometimes we don't realize that there are consequences for sinning.

When we sin; we are literally causing our own self-destruction. God does not do it . . . . we ourselves continue in our sins and therefore cause our own destruction. I will never forget when the LORD, showed me this.

It can make us physically sick or even cause physical or spiritual death. (Spiritual death means separation from God for eternity.) We can prevent this separation by turning from our sins and asking God to forgive us. The Bible tells us that God will forgive and forget our sins, but we ourselves are not always able to forget.

Even though we will be rescued from a spiritual death, we still must live with the consequences of our sin. That will serve as a reminder to us of our disobedience of God's laws. Could it be that this reminder is meant to persuade us against further sins?

"For the wages of sin is death; but the gift of God is eternal life through Jesus Christ our Lord." (Romans 6: 23) KJV

In the earliest civilizations of the Old Testament, there were those that rejected God altogether and chose instead to worship a false god that was tangible . . . one that could be seen touched and held. To accomplish that, man began making idols that were merely statues of animals, objects of fertility, nature and the heavens. They were made of wood, stone, gold and silver in various sizes and shapes.

One example was when Moses stayed on the mountain top for so long that the people below persuaded Moses' brother, Aaron, a priest, to craft a golden calf as a substitute object of worship and god to lead them. The golden calf represented one of the many false gods of the Egyptians. That was an extremely serious violation of God's commandments. Such a violation called for God's immediate discipline and punishment. The result was that three thousand Israelites died in a single day. Even after God's swift and severe punishment, the people continued to worship idols. Sorcerers, witches and even priests got involved in an effort to make the idols "come alive." They started demanding that sacrifices be made to the false gods, even requiring people to sacrifice their children in the fire as a tribute to the pagan god, Molech. See *(Ezekiel 23: 37) KJV.*

Blessings or Curse

By choosing not to follow God's commandments, *we* will bring curses upon ourselves. These are called "divine curses," or they could be "generational curses" that can affect an entire family for many generations. Are there sicknesses or diseases, such as certain illnesses or addictive behaviors, which have been passed down through your family line?

On the other hand, if *we* choose to obey God's commandments, we will bring on and receive His "divine blessings," which could be material blessings, the blessings of good health, the ability to have children and many others. More information about blessings and curses will follow.

The Gift of Free Will

God, in His wisdom, has given man the gift of "free will," so that he has the freedom to make his **own decisions** about following God and His Laws. God will not force us to have a relationship with Him, even though He longs for our love and worship. Sadly, it was the gift of free will that initially led to man's downfall in the Garden of Eden, when Adam and Eve disobeyed God's commands and lost their close relationship with Him.

Remember you can say "I will serve God" and keep His Laws or I can say "I will not serve Him." It's entirely up to you!

With great interest, I read the Book of Genesis, Chapters 19 and 20, and realized that they taught holy reverence for God. The first four Commandments taught me that Idolatry is absolutely forbidden. As I meditated on those chapters, I believe that God gave me a special revelation about the seriousness of His commandments.

The Conclusion

Before you begin reading the Ten Commandments for yourself, be sure to ask God's Holy Spirit to give you an understanding of the Scriptures. From my own experience, I know that it helps to ask God to open up His Word to you, and He will.

As for me, I will continue to believe in God's laws, by faith, and try my best to follow them. Hopefully, you will choose to do the same thing.

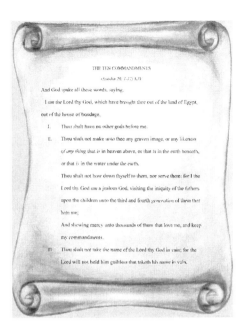

(Page 1)

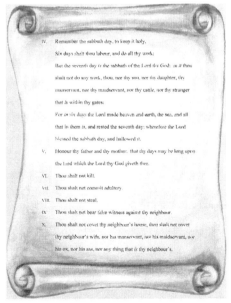

(Page 2)

THE TEN COMMANDMENTS

97

THE TEN COMMANDMENTS

Exodus 20: 1-17 (KJV)

And God spake all these words, saying,

I *am* the Lord thy God, which have brought thee out of the land of Egypt, out of the house of bondage.

I.   Thou shalt have no other gods before me.

II.   Thou shalt not make unto thee any graven image, or any likeness *of anything* that *is* in heaven above, or that *is* in the earth beneath, or that *is* in the water under the earth.

     Thou shalt not bow down thyself to them, nor serve them: for I the Lord thy God *am* a jealous God, visiting the iniquity of the fathers upon the children unto the third and fourth *generation* of them that hate me; And shewing mercy unto thousands of them that love me, and keep my commandments.

III.   Thou shalt not take the name of the Lord thy God in vain; for the Lord will not hold him guiltless that taketh his name in vain.

IV.   Remember the Sabbath day, to keep it holy. Six days shalt thou labour, and do all thy work: But the seventh day *is* the Sabbath of the Lord thy God: *in it* thou shalt not do any work, thou, nor thy son, nor thy daughter, thy manservant, nor thy maidservant, nor thy cattle, nor thy stranger that *is* within thy gates: For *in* six days the Lord made heaven and earth, the sea, and all that in them *is*, and rested the seventh day: wherefore the Lord blessed the Sabbath day, and hallowed it.

V.   Honour thy father and thy mother: that thy days may be long upon the land which the Lord thy God giveth thee.

VI.   Thou shalt not kill (Murder)

VII. Thou shalt not commit adultery.

VIII. Thou shalt not steal.

IX.   Thou shalt not bear false witness against thy neighbor.

X.   Thou shalt not covet thy neighbour's house; thou shalt not covet thy neighbour's wife, nor his manservant, nor his maidservant, nor his ox, nor his ass, nor any thing that *is* thy neighbour's.

CHAPTER 6

THE ORIGIN OF THE
"MISSING LINK"

The History of Ancient Religious Worship

The religion of Judaism began with the day that God spoke to Abraham. God was pleased with Abraham because he took God at His word and was obedient to Him. God asked him to leave his homeland and go to a place that He would show him.

"And I will make of thee, and a great nation and I will bless thee, and make thy name great: and thou shalt be a blessing: And I will bless them that bless thee, and curse him that curseth thee; and in thee shall all the families of the earth be blessed". (Genesis 12: 2-3) KJV

The reason he was asked to leave his homeland was because that region was full of idol worshippers, including Terah, his own father. God was not pleased with idol worship. He had established a different plan for mankind before the foundation of the earth and it would start with Abraham. Idol worship was common in the ancient world. People believed in many different gods. They even made sacrifices of their children to the god, Molech. Their gods were very demanding and unpredictable and they had no authentic source for their supposed power. Their priests would predict the future, say whether or not a god was pleased and require various offerings. As a result, they could influence the affairs of the people for good or evil.

You may remember the Old Testament story of the Israelites who had followed Joseph into Egypt because of a famine. There the Egyptians made slaves of them. So, they cried out to God for help and God heard their cries. God delivered them through a series of miraculous events.

After they left Egypt, God led them through the desert to Mt. Sinai. There they camped at the foot of the mountain. Moses ascended the mountain and met with God, where he was given the Ten Commandments. God said the people were to obey His commandments so that they could become holy, as He was holy. They were to worship no other god but Him or bow down to images of other gods. It was His guide for living and obeying the commandments that would prevent them from falling into idol worship. Below are the first four commandments:

"And God spake all these words, saying,

*I **am** the Lord thy God, which have brought thee out of the land of Egypt, out of the house of bondage.*

1. *Thou shalt have no other gods before me.*

2. *Thou shalt not make unto thee any graven image, or any likeness **of anything** that **is** in heaven above, or that **is** in the earth beneath, or that **is** in the water under the earth*

3. *Thou shalt not bow down thyself to them, nor serve them: for I the Lord thy God **am** a jealous God, visiting the iniquity of the fathers upon the children unto the third and fourth **generation** of them that hate me;*

4. *And showing mercy unto thousands of them that love me, and keep my commandments." (Exodus 20: 1-6) KJV*

Because Moses stayed on the mountain top with God for forty days, the people down below became very impatient and discouraged. At that point, they asked Aaron, their priest and brother of Moses, to make another god for them to worship. Out of fear, Aaron took offerings of gold from the people and created a golden calf, the symbol of an Egyptian god. God considered that a grave sin and He immediately sent Moses down the mountain to confront Aaron and the people. Because of their disobedience, the people were forced to wander in the desert for forty years before reaching Canaan, the land God had promised them. However, they would continue to be tempted to worship other gods, as they had freely done in Egypt.

When the Israelites finally reached Canaan, they were reminded to have nothing to do with the Canaanite gods. One of the Canaanite gods was Baal. The Canaanites, Egyptians, Babylonians, Assyrians, Greeks and Romans all believed that their man-made gods had supernatural powers.

Ordinary people worshipped at small, local shrines or chapels at the gateways of the great temples. Their worship consisted mostly of offerings and following certain sets of rituals. Only the priests entered the great state temples. They were the only ones who personally saw their pagan idols, which they claimed were gods. The rest of the people saw the idols only on festival days when their veiled images were carried outside of the temple by their priests in a procession.

When I learned these facts about the Ten Commandments and the prevalent idol worship of the day, it really opened my eyes to why my family would not worship in the Roman Catholic Church, the only church that existed in the Territory. I began to realize that this had been an unspoken problem my ancestors may have had for many years. They had embraced Messianic Judaism and understood that they were to be faithful to God's commandments. That is clearly why they were so uncomfortable with the practices of the church, as you will see later.

Let me remind you that the first believers in Yeshua (Jesus) as Messiah were Jews and they established the foundation of the Christian church. At first, Roman Catholics in that area seemed to believe the same, so it appeared that their doctrine was identical.

However, the early Roman Catholics in our community did begin to place religious statues in their churches that were made by local men, not long after they started. The statues were carvings of Jesus on the cross; Mary, the mother of Jesus; His disciples and various patron saints. It seemed very appropriate at the time. However, my family was keenly aware of God's laws forbidding the worship of religious images and idols. Because they read their Bibles, they knew they would be sinning by bowing down to man-made statues. Of course, this soon became a point of conflict and disagreement between friends and even some extended family members. Today, it is still somewhat of a problem. As I see it, this is where the persecution began and many families split, causing some to become secretive about their beliefs.

As I began to read in the Bible, I was amazed that even some kings in the Old Testament were involved in idol worship because they had married foreign women and began worshipping their pagan gods.

Every time I would read *"and they did evil in the sight of the Lord,"* it referred to the people going after other gods to serve them. Why did they do this? The Bible clearly tells us that such idols cannot see, hear, talk, think or move because they are man-made and are powerless.

Any time in Scripture that you see the phrase, *"and they did evil in the sight of the Lord,"* it usually means that the Israelites had rebelled against God's commandments and were worshipping idols and chasing after other gods. You can read about this yourself in the Old Testament Books of First and Second Kings.

A Better Appreciation:

As a result of my study, I came to a better understanding about my ancestors.

I realized that they were humble, and a very strong people. Their belief in God, was amazing. They tried to serve God with all of their heart. They had determined to be obedient to God regardless of the consequences.

Although, they sometimes still tried to be participating members of the local church outwardly, secretly, they continued to observe their Jewish traditions, just as they had always done. They even studied their Bible regularly, although laymen were forbidden by the ancient church traditions at that time to read Scriptures for themselves.

As a result of their Bible study, they finally chose to follow the apostolic beliefs and practices of Jesus and His disciples who established the first century congregations (churches). I don't know just how or when they decided; all I know is that they could no longer deny their conscience, after having learned the truth for themselves.

It seems that even then God was preparing our family for future opportunities and responsibilities. It wasn't long before God called my father to be the pastor of our small congregation of Messianic Jewish believers. It was the only congregation of its kind at that time in the area where we lived. Also, our religious education continued at home. My parents required all children under their supervision to memorize Scriptures, which we recited at the dinner table.

Another important assignment we were given was to memorize the "Shema," which was, and still is, a declaration of the central beliefs of our Messianic Jewish family and all others who have accepted Jesus as their Messiah.

"Hear, O Israel: The Lord our God is one Lord: And thou shalt love the Lord thy God with all thine heart, and with all thy soul, and with all thy might. And these words, which I command thee this day, shall be in thine heart: And thou shalt teach them diligently unto thy children, and shalt talk of them when thou sittest in thine house, and when thou walkest by the way, and when thou liest down, and when thou risest up. And thou shalt bind them for a sign upon thine hand, and they shall be as frontlets between thine eyes. And thou shalt write them on the posts of thy house, and on thy gate. (Deuteronomy 6: 4-9) KJV

Our parents taught us that if we obeyed God's commandments, as stated in the Ten Commandments, it would result in God's blessings. However, if we rebelled and disobeyed His commandments, we would bring curses upon ourselves and even upon our families after we were married.

Once this information was revealed to me by older family members, then I could appreciate how difficult it must have been for my ancestors not only to keep their Messianic beliefs intact down through many generations, but to pass that knowledge on to their descendants.

Finally, I felt that I had unlocked the mystery of why events had unfolded the way they did. This revelation will continue to be of great value to future generations. This information may not be accepted by church historians, but I am only speaking about my own family's experiences. I was able to confirm in God's Holy Word why my ancestors' beliefs in the one true Living God, the importance of obeying His commandments against idol worship, and the scriptural revelation of Yeshua (Jesus) as Messiah were so important to them. I had privately wondered about the gap between our Messianic beliefs and the religious beliefs of others. When I finally understood it, I called this gap the "Missing Link."

I am humbled as I write about this revelation and the mystery surrounding it. It is not my intention to hurt anyone's feelings or to criticize them or their religious beliefs. I am only writing my views on what I think happened during those early years.

I am not an expert in any church doctrine. When I teach Sunday school, I teach directly from the Bible, along with other helps, such as Bible Dictionaries, Encyclopedias and other religious writings that I think will help me to interpret and rightly divide the Word of Truth. I am writing this as a layman and not as a scholar in any religious field.

My intention is to offer a better understanding of the beliefs of our Sephardic Messianic Jewish family. There are many misunderstandings about church doctrine that can be interpreted in negative ways. It is clear that there are indisputable differences between different church beliefs. In my heart, I believe that each person is born with a basic desire to know God. Those who accept Him want to be as Biblically correct and obedient as possible.

My heart's desire is to answer the many questions that arise causing negative attitudes toward the Messianic Jewish believers who settled in New Mexico and Colorado. Those believers have always been a very private people and they have survived many persecutions in their history. They are a devout and strong people and I am honored to call them "my people." God alone knows the purpose for this book and its timing. I believe it will soon be revealed.

CHAPTER 6

PART ONE

DIVINE CURSES

(Deuteronomy 27: 15-26) KJV

Starting in God's Word with Verse 15:

15. Cursed *be* the man that maketh *any* graven or molten image, an abomination unto the Lord, the work of the hands of the craftsman, and putteth *it* in *a* secret *place*. And all the people shall answer and say, Amen.

16. Cursed *be* he that setteth light [dishonors] by his father or his mother. And all the people shall say, Amen.

17. Cursed *be* he that removeth his neighbour's landmark. And all the people shall say, Amen.

18. Cursed *be* he that maketh the blind to wander out of the way. And all the people shall say, Amen.

19. Cursed *be* he that perverteth [withholds justice] the judgment of the stranger, fatherless, and widow. And all the people shall say, Amen.

20. Cursed *be* he that lieth with his father's wife; because he uncovereth [dishonors] his father's skirt. And all the people shall say, Amen

21. Cursed *be* he that lieth with any manner of beast. And all the people shall say, Amen.

22. Cursed *be* he that lieth with his sister, the daughter of his father, or the daughter of his mother. And all the people shall say, Amen.

23. Cursed *be* he that lieth with his mother in law. And all the people shall say, Amen.

24. Cursed *be* he that smiteth [kills] his neighbor secretly. And all the people shall say, Amen.

25. Cursed *be* he that taketh reward to slay an innocent person. And all the people shall say, Amen.

26. Cursed *be* he that confirmeth not [does not uphold] all the words of this law to do them. And all the people shall say, Amen.

CHAPTER 6

PART TWO:

DIVINE CURSES

(Deuteronomy 28: 14-68) KJV

Starting in God's Word with Verse 14:

14. And thou shalt not go aside from any of the **words** which I command thee this day, *to* the right hand, or *to* the left, to go after other gods to serve them.

15. But it shall come to pass, if thou wilt not hearken unto the voice of the LORD thy God, to observe to do all his commandments and his statutes which I command thee this day; that all these curses shall come upon thee, and overtake thee:

16. Cursed *shalt* thou *be* in the city, and cursed *shalt* thou *be* in the field.

17. Cursed *shall be* thy basket and thy store.

18. Cursed *shall be* the fruit of thy body, and the fruit of thy land, the increase of thy kine, and the flocks of thy sheep.

19. Cursed *shalt* thou *be* when thou comest in, and cursed *shalt* thou *be* when thou goest out.

20. The LORD shall send upon thee cursing, vexation, and rebuke, in all that thou settest thine hand unto for to do, until thou be destroyed, and until thou perish quickly; because of the wickedness of thy doings, whereby thou hast forsaken me.

21. The LORD shall make the pestilence cleave unto thee, until he have consumed thee from off the land; whither thou goest to possess it.

22. The LORD shall smite thee with a consumption, and with a fever, and with an inflammation, and with an extreme burning, and with the sword, and with blasting, and with mildew; and they shall pursue thee until thou perish.

23. And thy heaven that *is* over thy head shall be brass, and the earth that is under thee *shall be* iron.

24. The LORD shall make the rain of thy land powder and dust: from heaven shall it come down upon thee, until thou be destroyed.

25. The LORD shall cause thee to be smitten before thine enemies: thou shalt go out one way against them, and flee seven ways before them: and shalt be removed into all the kingdoms of the earth.

26. And thy carcase shall be meat unto all fowls of the air, and unto the beasts of the earth, and no man shall fray *them* away.

27. The LORD will smite thee with the botch of Egypt, and with the emerods, and with the scab, and with the itch, whereof thou canst not be healed.

28. The LORD shall smite thee with madness, and blindness, and astonishment of heart:

29. And thou shalt grope at noonday, as the blind gropeth in darkness, and thou shalt not prosper in thy ways: and thou shalt be only oppressed and spoiled evermore, and no man shall save *thee*.

30. Thou shalt betroth a wife, and another man shall lie with her:

thou shalt build an house, and thou shalt not dwell therein: thou shalt plant a vineyard, and shalt not gather the grapes thereof.

31. Thine ox *shall be* slain before thine eyes, and thou shalt not eat thereof: thine ass *shall be* violently taken away from before thy face, and shall not be restored to thee: thy sheep *shall be* given to thine enemies, and thou shalt have none to rescue *them*.

32. Thy sons and thy daughters *shall be* given unto another people, and thine eyes shall look, and fail *with longing* for them all the day long: and *there shall be* no might in thine hand.

33. The fruit of thy land, and all thy labours, shall a nation which thou knowest not eat up; and thou shalt be only oppressed and crushed alway:

34. So that thou shalt be mad for the sight of thine eyes which thou shalt see.

35. The LORD shall smite thee in the knees, and in the legs, with a sore botch that cannot be healed, from the sole of thy foot unto the top of thy head.

36. The LORD shall bring thee, and thy king which thou shalt set over thee, unto a nation which neither thou nor thy fathers have known; and there shalt thou serve other gods, wood and stone.

37. And thou shalt become an astonishment, a proverb, and a byword; among all nations whither the LORD shall lead thee.

38. Thou shalt carry much seed out into the field, and shalt gather *but* little in; for the locust shall consume it.

39. Thou shalt plant vineyards, and dress *them*, but shalt neither drink *of* the wine, nor gather *the grapes*; for the worms shall eat them.

40. Thou shalt have olive trees throughout all thy coasts, but thou shalt not anoint *thyself* with the oil; for thine olive shall cast *his* fruit.

41. Thou shalt beget sons and daughters, but thou shalt not enjoy them; for they shall go into captivity.

42. All thy trees and fruit of thy land shall the locust consume.

43. The stranger that *is* within thee shall get up above thee very high; and thou shalt come down very low.

44. He shall lend to thee, and thou shalt not lend to him: he shall be the head, and thou shalt be the tail.

45. Moreover all these curses shall come upon thee, and shall pursue thee, and overtake thee, till thou be destroyed; because thou hearkenedst not unto the voice of the LORD thy God, to keep his commandments and his statutes which he commanded thee.

46. And they shall be upon thee for a sign and for a wonder, and upon thy seed for ever.

47. Because thou servedst not the LORD thy God with joyfulness, and with gladness of heart, for the abundance of all *things*;

48. Therefore shalt thou serve thine enemies which the LORD shall send against thee, in hunger, and in thirst, and in nakedness, and in want of all *things*: and he shall put a yoke of iron upon thy neck, until he have destroyed thee.

49. The LORD shall bring a nation against thee from far, from the end of the earth, *as swift* as the eagle flieth; a nation whose tongue thou shalt not understand;

50. A nation of fierce countenance, which shall not regard the person of the old, nor shew favour to the young:

51. And he shall eat the fruit of thy cattle, and the fruit of thy land, until thou be destroyed: which *also* shall not leave thee *either* corn, wine, or oil, *or* the increase of thy kine, or flocks of thy sheep, until he have destroyed thee.

52. And he shall besiege thee in all thy gates, until thy high and fenced walls come down, wherein thou trustedst, throughout all thy land: and he shall besiege thee in all thy gates throughout all thy land, which the LORD thy God hath given thee.

53. And thou shalt eat the fruit of thine own body, the flesh of thy sons and of thy daughters, which the LORD thy God hath given thee, in the siege, and in the straitness, wherewith thine enemies shall distress thee:

54. So *that* the man *that* is tender among you, and very delicate, his eye shall be evil toward his brother, and toward the wife of his bosom, and toward the remnant of his children which he shall leave:

55. So that he will not give to any of them of the flesh of his children whom he shall eat: because he hath nothing left him in the siege, and in the straitness, wherewith thine enemies shall distress thee in all thy gates.

56. The tender and delicate woman among you, which would not adventure to set the sole of her foot upon the ground for delicateness and tenderness, her eye shall be evil toward the husband of her bosom, and toward her son, and toward her daughter,

57. And toward her young one that cometh out from between her feet, and toward her children which she shall bear: for she shall eat them for want of all *things* secretly in the siege and straitness, wherewith thine enemy shall distress thee in thy gates.

58. If thou wilt not observe to do all the words of this law that are written in this book, that thou mayest fear this glorious and fearful name, THE LORD THY GOD;

59. Then the LORD will make thy plagues wonderful, and the plagues of thy seed, *even* great plagues, of long continuance, and sore sicknesses, and of long continuance.

60. Moreover, he will bring upon thee all the diseases of Egypt, which thou wast afraid of; and they shall cleave unto thee.

61. Also every sickness, and every plague, which *is* not written in the book of this law, them will the LORD bring upon thee, until thou be destroyed.

62. And ye shall be left few in number, whereas ye were as the stars of heaven for multitude; because thou wouldest not obey the voice of the LORD thy God.

63. And it shall come to pass, *that* as the LORD rejoiced over you to do you good, and to multiply you; so the LORD will rejoice over you to destroy you, and to bring you to nought; and ye shall be plucked from off the land whither thou goest to possess it.

64. And the LORD shall scatter thee among all people, from the one end of the earth even until the other; and there thou shalt serve other gods, which neither thou nor thy fathers have known, *even* wood and stone.

65. And among these nations shalt thou find no ease, neither shall the sole of thy foot have rest: but the LORD shall give thee there a trembling heart, and failing of eyes, and sorrow of mind;

66. And thy life shall hang in doubt before thee; and thou shalt fear day and night, and shalt have none assurance of thy life:

67. In the morning thou shalt say, Would God it were even! And at even thou shalt say, Would God it were morning! for the fear of thine heart wherewith thou shalt fear, and for the sight of thine eyes which thou shalt see.

68. And the LORD shall bring thee into Egypt again with ships, by the way whereof I spake unto thee, Thou shalt see it no more again: and there ye shall be sold unto your enemies for bondmen and bondwomen, and no man shall buy *you*.

CHAPTER 6

DIVINE BLESSINGS

(Deuteronomy 28: 1-14) KJV

1. And it shall come to pass, if thou shalt hearken diligently unto the voice of the Lord thy God, to observe *and* to do all his commandments, which I command thee this day, that the LORD thy God will set thee on high above all nations of the earth:

2. And all these blessings shall come on thee, and overtake thee, if thou shalt hearken unto the voice of the LORD thy God.

3. Blessed *shalt* thou *be* in the city, and blessed *shalt* thou *be* in the field.

4. Blessed *shall be* the fruit of thy body, and the fruit of thy ground, and the fruit of thy cattle, the increase of thy kine, and the flocks of thy sheep.

5. Blessed *shall be* thy basket and thy store.

6. Blessed *shalt* thou *be* when thou comest in, and blessed *shalt* thou *be* when thou goest out.

7. The LORD shall cause thine enemies that rise up against thee to be smitten before thy face: they shall come out against thee one way, and flee before thee seven ways.

8. The LORD shall command the blessing upon thee in thy storehouses, and in all that thou settest thine hand unto; and he shall bless thee in the land which the LORD thy God giveth thee.

9. The LORD shall establish thee an holy people unto Himself, as he hath sworn unto thee, if thou shalt keep the commandments of the LORD thy God, and walk in his ways.

10. And all the people of the earth shall see that thou art called by the name of the LORD; and they shall be afraid of thee.

11. And the LORD shall make thee plenteous in goods, in the fruit of thy body, and in the fruit of thy cattle, and in the fruit of thy ground, in the land which the LORD sware unto thy fathers to give thee.

12. The LORD shall open unto thee his good treasure, the heaven to give the rain unto thy land in his season, and to bless all the work of thine hand: and thou shalt lend unto many nations, and thou shalt not borrow.

13. And the LORD shall make thee the head, and not the tail; and thou shalt be above only, and thou shall not be beneath; if that thou hearken unto the commandments of the LORD thy God, which I command thee this day, to observe and to do *them*:

14. And thou shalt not go aside from any of the **words** which I command thee this day, *to* the right hand, or *to* the left, to go after other gods to serve them.

CHAPTER 7

HOLIDAYS

The Feast of Passover—Yeshua (Jesus)

"The Passover Lamb"

The Feast of Rosh HaShanah—The Jewish New Year

"Shofar—the Ram's Horn"

Hanukkah (Chanukah)—The Feast of Dedication

and The Feast of Lights

"The Menorah"

CHAPTER 7

THE FEAST OF PASSOVER

YESHUA (JESUS),
OUR PASSOVER LAMB

(Isaiah 53: 7; John 1: 29; 1 Peter 1: 19; Luke 22: 1 ;)
(Revelation 7: 9-10; Revelation 15: 3-4; Revelation 21: 22-23) KJV

THE INNOCENT LAMB THAT TOOK AWAY THE SINS OF
MANKIND FOREVER

CHAPTER 7

THE FEAST OF PASSOVER

EXODUS 12: 14

Yeshua, our Passover Lamb

"On the fourteenth day of the first month the Lord's Passover is to be held. On the fifteenth day of this month there is to be a festival; for seven days eat bread made without yeast." (Numbers 28: 16-17) NIV

Every year, on the fourteenth day of the first month of the Jewish calendar, the Lord's Passover, or Pesach (Hebrew), is to be observed. It commemorates the day on or about 1500 B.C. when God, by His great power, delivered the Israelites from 400 years of Egyptian slavery. He had allowed the Israelites to be taken captive as punishment for idol worship and rebellion. (Exodus 12: 1-36 and Numbers 28:16-25) NIV [New International Version]

In order to accomplish their deliverance, God sent ten plagues on the Egyptians. Pharaoh, the Egyptian ruler, refused to release the Israelites until the time of the final plague when the Lord caused the death of the firstborn child and firstborn animal of every Egyptian family in the land. Not surprisingly, after that, Pharaoh told their Jewish leader, Moses, to take his people and go.

In order to protect the Israelites' firstborn child and firstborn animal from death, the Lord instructed every Israelite family to kill a lamb and place its blood on the top and sides of their door frame, *[this forms a cross]*. The Lord would see the blood and pass over that home.

"For I will pass through the land of Egypt this night, and will smite all the firstborn in the land of Egypt, both man and beast; and against all the gods of Egypt I will execute judgment:

I am the Lord.

And the blood shall be to you for a token upon the houses where ye are: and when I see the blood, I will pass over you, and the plague shall not be upon you to destroy you, when I smite the land of Egypt." (Exodus 12: 12-13) KJV

Each Israelite family was told to cook and eat their meal in haste, so they could leave Egypt quickly. They were to eat unleavened bread, Matzah, which wouldn't have time to rise, and bitter herbs, representing their hasty departure and the bitterness of slavery. In scripture, leaven is symbolic of sin. *(Leviticus 6: 17) NIV*

To commemorate when the Lord passed over the homes of the Israelites, the event became known as the "Passover." From that time to the present, Passover is remembered each spring with a celebratory meal called "The Seder" (Order of Events).

At the meal, the Old Testament story of the Passover is re-told, which re-telling is called "The Haggadah."

Sacrificing a lamb at Passover was nothing new to the Israelites, because for centuries God had required each family to sacrifice a lamb annually as atonement for sin.

"In fact we can say that under the old agreement almost everything was cleansed by sprinkling it with blood, and without the shedding of blood there is no forgiveness of sins." (Hebrews 9:22) TLB [The Living Bible]

Each year all Israelite males were required to bring a first-born lamb, without blemish, to the priest as a burnt offering and atonement for the sins of his family. The lamb was then slain and its blood was sprinkled on the altar. Because it would cover their sins for only one year, the sacrifice had to be repeated again and again.

To carry out God's commandment, the people came to Jerusalem on the day before the Passover celebration and immediately purchased their lambs. Next, the head of each household would bring his lamb into the temple courtyard. There, in the presence of the Priest, he would slay his lamb. Then he would take it home in order to prepare the Passover meal. During the meal, it was customary to dip the bitter herbs in salt water to remember the bitterness of slavery in Egypt. Another symbolic ritual was the use of Matzah, which represented the promise of the hoped for Jewish Messiah.

Once the Israelites were delivered from Egypt, they entered the wilderness and Passover became an annual celebration. They also observed a second feast in connection with Passover called the "Feast of Unleavened Bread." God instructed the people to eat unleavened bread for seven days. Later on, Passover and the Feast of Unleavened Bread were merged into one holiday. *(Exodus 12: 8, 15; Exodus 13: 3, 6-7) KJV*

There is another Old Testament story that deserves re-telling. One day God commanded his faithful servant, Abraham, to sacrifice his only son, Isaac. This son was the fulfillment of God's promise to Abraham that he would have a child even though he was 100 years old at the time. God instructed Abraham to bring Isaac to Mount Mariah and sacrifice him there. Think how Abraham must have felt when God told him to sacrifice his beloved son. Nevertheless, Abraham proceeded to follow God's instructions; and, at the last minute, God provided a ram to sacrifice in the place of Isaac.

We are amazed at Abraham's willingness to obey God's command. We are even more amazed that God the Father would sacrifice His only begotten son, Yeshua (Jesus) on the cross for the redemption of all mankind. We must realize that God's eternal plan has always been centered on Yeshua (Jesus) and the revelation of who He is.

400 Years Later

Four hundred years later, God introduced a New Covenant (New Testament). That was when God sent Yeshua (Jesus), His only begotten Son, to earth to fulfill His eternal plan for the redemption of mankind. That eternal plan had been in place from the foundation of the earth. Yeshua's (Jesus') earthly ministry lasted for three years.

At the end of His earthly ministry, on the night preceding His death on the cross, we find Yeshua (Jesus) celebrating the Passover meal with His disciples in Jerusalem. The Bible describes that night when Yeshua (Jesus) the Messiah had gathered with His disciples in an Upper Room for the purpose of leading them in a Seder. At one point, He explained to them that after they had completed their Passover meal, He would be betrayed and die. *(Luke 22: 20-22) KJV*

As He passed the food, He explained the mystery of God's plan of redemption and introduced God's New Covenant (New Testament). When He broke the bread and gave thanks, He told His disciples,

"This is my body given for you; do this in remembrance of me." (Luke 22:19) KJV

When He lifted the cup of wine, He acknowledged that it represented His blood. Just as the blood of a lamb brought atonement for sins to the Israelites, likewise our Messiah's blood and atoning death would bring salvation to all those who believe in Him.

"And he took the cup, and gave thanks, and said, Take this and divide it among yourselves:

For I say unto you, I will not drink of the fruit of the vine, until the kingdom of God shall come."

(Luke 22: 17-18) KJV

As a part of the Seder, there are four cups of wine. Jesus explained that they represent the four steps of God's plan of redemption and the restoration of man's relationship with God that was broken in the Garden of Eden.

The **first cup** is the *Cup of Sanctification*, meaning "to separate." It is our faith in Yeshua (Jesus the Messiah) that sanctifies us and separates us to live holy lives:

"Sanctify yourselves therefore, and be ye holy: for I am the Lord your God."

(Leviticus 20: 7) KJV

The **second cup** is the *Cup of Deliverance* and *Cup of Thanksgiving*, which is based on God's promise to Israel:

"Wherefore say unto the children of Israel, I am the Lord, and I will bring you out from under the burdens of the Egyptians, and I will rid you out of their bondage, and I will redeem you with an outstretched arm, and with great judgments." (Exodus 6:6) KJV

Messianic Jews believe their own deliverance is freedom from the bondage of sin.

The **third cup** is the *Cup of Redemption*, which refers to the fulfillment of God's promise to Moses that He would free His people from Egyptian slavery:

"And he took the cup, and when he had given thanks, he gave it to them: and they all drank of it.

And he said unto them, This is my blood of the New Testament [new covenant], which is shed for many."

(Mark 14: 23-24) KJV

"And he took the cup, and gave thanks, and gave it to them, saying, Drink ye all of it;

For this is my blood of the New Testament [new covenant], which is shed for many for the remission of sins." (Matthew 26: 27-28) KJV

The **fourth and final cup** is the *Cup of Praise and Worship* and the *Cup of Completion,* also known as the *Cup of the Kingdom,* or *"Hallel,"* meaning praise and worship. It is based upon God's promise that, *"I will take you as my own people, and I will be your God: (Exodus 6:7) NIV*

Christians call this Upper Room meal the "Last Supper" or "Communion."

After Yeshua (Jesus) and His disciples finished eating, they left the Upper Room and departed for the Mount of Olives.

"And when they had sung a hymn, they went out into the Mount of Olives." (Matthew 26: 30) KJV

As Yeshua (Jesus) predicted, He was soon betrayed, beaten and sacrificed on a cross [tree], thus becoming the *sacrificial lamb* of the New Testament. His sacrificial death as the "Lamb of God", did, in fact, take away the sins of the world once and for all. He is the final atonement for the sins of all those who believe in Him.

It was no coincidence that Yeshua (Jesus) was dying on the cross at the same time that a lamb would have been sacrificed for the sins of the Israelites in the Old Testament.

The prophets had prophesied long before about Yeshua (Jesus). The Holy Scriptures are very clear about the prophecies regarding Yeshua (Jesus) and His death on the cross.

"He was oppressed, and he was afflicted, yet he opened not his mouth: he is brought as a lamb to the slaughter, and as a sheep before her shearers is dumb, so he opened not his mouth." (Isaiah 53: 7) KJV

I would like to explain Passover from the viewpoint of a Messianic believer. Most of us strictly believe that the Passover feast is to be celebrated throughout all generations, a covenant which every believer should observe. Yeshua (Jesus) set an example for us by faithfully observing Passover Himself.

All too often, we have read the scriptures about Passover; but, without asking God for His revelation and without background knowledge of the Old Testament, we can miss its true meaning. *(Exodus 12) KJV*

However, if we have that knowledge, we can understand why the (Matzah) bread is symbolic of Yeshua's (Jesus') body. The Old Testament prophet, Isaiah, tells us,

"But he was wounded for our transgressions; he was bruised for our iniquities: the chastisement of our peace was upon him; and with his stripes we are healed." (Isaiah 53: 5) KJV

Today, preparation for Passover begins days earlier when all items containing leaven or yeast are removed from the home. It is a time when we examine our hearts and commit to remove all hidden sin. Once we are cleansed of sin, we may fully participate in the miraculous transition from the slavery of sin to the freedom of God's forgiveness and mercy.

Today the feast, or Seder, takes place in the home. The order of the meal is based upon the directives God gave in scripture. He told the Israelites to always include three things: lamb, Matzah and bitter herbs. *(Exodus 12) NIV*

Rabbis later added other items to the meal, including green vegetables, a roasted egg, Charoset (apple-nut mixture) and four cups of wine. The wine used for the meal represents the blood of the innocent lamb slain for the atonement of sins and the Seder Plate is a symbolic representation of the entire story of God's redemptive plan.

The service begins with the lighting of a candle. A woman is chosen to light the candle, as she pronounces a blessing, because it was a woman who brought forth Yeshua (Jesus), the Light of the World. He was born as our redeemer and the promised seed of a virgin. *(Isaiah 7: 14) KJV*

The Passover meal always includes the re-telling of the original Passover story; and, during the meal, children ask four specific questions and are given answers as to why certain steps are being taken.

In our Seder celebration, the leader reads and tells us that Elijah (the Old Testament prophet) did not see death, but was swept up to heaven in a chariot of fire by a great whirlwind. Most Jews believe that Elijah will return during a Passover celebration to announce the coming of the Jewish Messiah, Son of David. Messianic Jews believe that Yeshua (Jesus) is the promised Messiah who has already come, as proven by His birth, death and resurrection from the dead. We also believe that He will return again at a future date, in an event called "The Rapture" or "The Gathering." *(I Thessalonians 4: 13-18) KJV*

At the Seder, an extra place is set for Elijah and a child is sent to the door to symbolically welcome Elijah to the Seder.

"See, I will send you the prophet Elijah before that great and dreadful day of the Lord comes." (Malachi 4:5) NIV

Is it possible that Elijah has already returned? In the New Testament story of John the Baptist, an angel prophesied before his birth that he would prepare the way for the Lord's earthly ministry.

"And he will go on before the Lord, in the spirit and power of Elijah, to turn the hearts of the fathers to their children and the disobedient to the wisdom of the righteous—to make ready a people prepared for the Lord." (Luke 1: 17) NIV

Jesus Himself spoke of John the Baptist, saying

"And if you are willing to accept it, he is the Elijah who was to come." (Matthew 11: 14) NIV

It was John the Baptist, who first announced the arrival of Yeshua (Jesus) and declared, *"The next day John saw Jesus coming toward him and said, Look, the Lamb of God, who takes away the sin of the world!" (John 1:29) NIV*

For many Messianic Jewish families the Passover celebration ended with the singing of "Dayenu," a song of praise and worship.

The Passover service is concluded with everyone joyously shouting in unison, "NEXT YEAR IN JERUSALEM!"

CHAPTER 7

THE FEAST OF ROSH HASHANAH
THE JEWISH NEW YEAR

Shofar—The Ram's Horn

(Leviticus 23: 23-25) KJV

CHAPTER 7

THE FEAST OF ROSH HASHANAH
THE JEWISH NEW YEAR

Historical Background

"And the Lord spake unto Moses, saying,

*Speak unto the children of Israel, saying, in the seventh month, in the **first** day of the month, shall ye have a sabbath, a memorial of blowing of trumpets, an holy convocation.*

*Ye shall do no servile work **therein**: but ye shall offer an offering made by fire unto the Lord." (Leviticus 23: 23-25) KJV*

The feast of "Rosh HaShanah" is also called "The Jewish New Year," "Head of the Year," and the "Day of the Sounding of Trumpets" (Yom Teruah). The Jewish calendar always begins in the month of September. On the first day of the celebration, a loud trumpet is sounded. The Jewish version of a trumpet is actually a ram's horn called a "shofar." It is blown as a call for re-gathering. The trumpet, or shofar, blast is used to "call for a solemn assembly, to warn of danger and action to be taken," such as the gathering of troops for war. It can also herald and honor <u>the arrival and coronation of a king.</u> Rosh HaShanah has come to represent a day of repentance. In the Old Testament, it was the day when the people of Israel took stock of their spiritual condition and made the necessary changes to ensure that the upcoming New Year would be pleasing to God. It is still in practice today.

In synagogues, the Shofar or ram's horn is sounded once daily for an entire month to alert the faithful that the time for repentance has come.

Every Jewish holiday officially begins at sundown on the evening before the holiday. In keeping with the call to repentance and turning to God, Rosh HaShanah is always spent in worship, including music and prayer.

In traditional groups, the afternoon of Rosh HaShanah is spent at a body of water (ocean, lake or stream) observing the ancient service *Tashlich*. The word is derived from *(Micah 7: 19) KJV* where the prophet promises, " . . . thou [God] wilt cast all their sins into the depths of the sea." To illustrate this, people cast their bread crumbs or pebbles into the water and rejoice in God's promise of forgiveness.

My Point of view

As I was studying the history of Rosh HaShanah and the words of the Apostle Paul, I came to realize that the blowing of the trumpet could also announce the future Re-gathering of believers by Yeshua (Jesus), the Messiah, at an event called "The Rapture," the word Rapture is not in the English Bible, but the scripture is very clear. KJV

*"For the Lord himself shall descend from heaven with a shout, with the voice of the archangel, and with the trump of God: and the dead in Christ shall rise first Then we which are alive **and** remain shall be caught up together with them in the clouds, to meet the Lord in the air: and so shall we ever be with the Lord.*

Wherefore comfort one another with these words."

(1 Thessalonians 4: 16-18) KJV

Paul also states in the New Testament:

"Now this I say, brethren, that flesh and blood cannot inherit the kingdom of God; neither doth corruption inherit incorruption.

Behold, I shew you a mystery; We shall not all sleep, but we shall all be changed,

In a moment, in the twinkling of an eye, at the last trump: for the trumpet shall sound, and the dead shall be raised incorruptible, and we shall be changed. For this corruptible must put on incorruption, and this mortal must put on immortality."

(I Corinthians 15: 50-52) KJV

All true believers in Yeshua (Jesus) are eagerly awaiting The Rapture. It will be a great and glorious day for believers; but, according to scripture, it will be a terrible day for those who have not believed God's Word, the "Bible." They will be left behind to go through "The Great Tribulation," which will last for seven years.

"For then shall be great tribulation, such as was not since the beginning of the world to this time, no, nor ever shall be.

And except those days should be shortened, there should no flesh be saved: but for the elect's sake those days shall be shortened." (Matthew 24: 21-22) KJV

There are ten days between Rosh HaShanah and the next celebration, which is "Yom Kippur." The ten days in between are called "The Days of Awe." They are days for prayer and fasting.

They provide a time for people to repent of their sins and seek forgiveness from those they may have harmed, so that restitution can be made. At the end of The Days of Awe, there is held a special celebratory dinner feast on Yom Kippur.

My Point of view

In my opinion, the special feast celebrated on Yom Kippur, could also refer to a future event in Heaven called "The Marriage Supper of the Lamb," described in the last book of the Bible, Revelation.

"Let us be glad and rejoice, and give honour to him: for the marriage of the Lamb [Yeshua (Jesus)] is come, and his wife [the church] hath made herself ready.

And to her was granted that she should be arrayed in fine linen, clean and white: for the fine linen is the righteousness of saints.

And he saith unto me [Apostle John], Write, Blessed are they which are called unto the marriage supper of the Lamb. And he saith unto me, These are the true sayings of God."

(Revelation 19:7—9) KJV

The Marriage Supper of the Lamb is a great day of rejoicing when Yeshua (Jesus) and His church, made up of Messianic Jews and Gentile believers all, those who believe and have trusted in the LORD, are united together.

Only the Father, Jehovah God Himself, knows for sure the day when Yeshua (Jesus) will come for His people. No one knows.

*"But of that day and hour knoweth no **man**, no, not the angels of heaven, but my Father only." (Matthew 24: 36) KJV*

"Watch therefore, for ye know neither the day nor the hour wherein the Son of man cometh." (Matthew 25: 13) KJV

"He which testifieth these things saith, Surely I come quickly.
Amen. Even so, come, Lord Jesus.
*The grace of our Lord Jesus Christ **be** with you all. Amen."*
(Revelation 22: 20-21) KJV.

From: "God's Appointed Times." By Barney Kasdan.
(Lederer Messianic Publications. Maryland: 1993).

CHAPTER 7

HANUKKAH (CHANUKAH)
THE FEAST OF DEDICATION AND
FEAST OF LIGHTS

The Feast of Hanukkah:
The Menorah
(John 10: 22-23) KJV

CHAPTER 7

HANUKKAH (CHANUKAH)

"The Feast of Dedication"

and

"The Feast of Lights"

(John 10: 22-23)

The story of Hanukkah goes back a century and a half before Yeshua (Jesus) was born in Bethlehem. At that time, Israel was being oppressed by the powerful King of Syria, Antiochus IV. At the same time, there was a conflict between the Ptolemaic Empire of Egypt and the Seleucid Empire of Syria. These two enemy leaders were about to fight each other, but decided instead to unite in battle against the Jews.

For some time, King Antiochus IV had thought that the Jews were being too loyal to their God, so he decided to change that. He required them to write on a ram's horn the words, "We have no portion in the God of Israel." He also forbade them from practicing circumcision, celebrating the biblically appointed feasts, worshipping on the Sabbath and reading the Torah.

To further infuriate the Jews, King Antiochus IV began to offer sacrifices to his pagan gods on the holy altar of God and he even sacrificed a pig on the altar, a tremendous insult to the Jews. He also erected in the temple a statue of Zeus Olympus, chief among the Greek gods, and even began using the sacred vessels. All of these practices were strictly forbidden by God. Finally, King Antiochus IV took on the title of "Epiphanies," which means "God Manifested."

This had the Jews extremely upset and on the 25th day of December, 168 B.C., the Jews revolted against the religious oppression. A high priest by the name of Mattilyhu and his son, Yhudah (Judah), from the Maccabaeus ("Hammer") family of Israel, formed an army to fight both the Egyptians and Syrians. Unfortunately, the combined army of their enemies was much larger and stronger, so they prayed to God for help. The Lord did help them to defeat their enemies and three years later the temple was restored. At that time, they joyfully celebrated the re-dedication of the temple and returned to their worship of God.

However, when the temple was restored, a serious problem occurred. There was an eight-branch Menorah used in the temple service that was required to be perpetually lighted and the light had gone out. They realized that they had just one jar of oil available, which would keep the Menorah lighted for only one day. That's when God performed a miracle and their one jar of oil lasted for eight days, giving the Israelites time to consecrate a new supply of oil for the Menorah.

The Nine Candle Menorah

On each night during Hanukkah, the ninth candle is used to light each of the eight candles on the Menorah, until all of the candles are lit. The ninth candle is called the "Shammas" or "Servant." Today, gifts are given daily for eight days of Hanukkah in remembrance of God's deliverance by the Maccabaeus and for the miracle of the oil that occurred at that time.

New Testament

In the New Testament, Yeshua (Jesus) represents the servant candle because He stated that He came not to be served, but to minister to others.

"But it shall not be so among you [his disciples]: but whosoever will be great among you, let him be your minister; And whosoever will be chief among you, let him be your servant: Even as the Son of man [Jesus] came not to be ministered unto, but to minister, and to give his life a ransom for many." (Matthew 20: 26-28) KJV

Yeshua (Jesus) is also referred to as to servant in the New Testament Book of Philippians:

"Who, being in the form of God, thought it not robbery to be Equal with God: But made himself of no reputation, and took upon him the form of a servant, and was made in the likeness of men:

And being found in fashion as a man, he humbled himself, and became obedient unto death, even the death of the cross." (Philippians 2: 6-8) KJV

When I was growing up, Hanukkah was one of the Messianic Jewish holidays that we celebrated privately. We didn't call it Hanukkah because the name Hanukkah was not mentioned in the Old Testament. There it is called both the "Feast of Dedication" and the "Feast of Lights." We had learned about the holiday and how to observe it from a story about the history of the Jewish people. I don't remember the exact date when we celebrated it, except that it was in December at Christmastime. We just called it a "Time for Lights," which celebration lasted for eight days. That's when the children got to enjoy brightly burning lights in the front yard at night. Most people called them luminaries. Also, our mother would prepare special food cooked in olive oil: potato pancakes, doughnuts, latkes and cookies shaped like stars.

The Feast of Lights

We learned that the existence of light began when God created the universe in the Old Testament Book of Genesis:

"And God said, Let there be light: and there was light.

And God saw the light, that is was good: and God divided the light from the darkness." (Genesis 1: 3-4) KJV

Centuries later, in *(Exodus 13: 21-22) KJV*, when the Israelites were wandering in the wilderness on their way to the "promised land," God provided their only source of light.

They were led by a pillar of cloud by day and a pillar of fire by night. That enabled them to travel by day or night.

In *(John 10:22-30) KJV*, there is a reference to the "Feast of Dedication," (Hanukkah). Yeshua (Jesus) used that occasion to declare that He was the Messiah of Israel and that He was deity.

"And it was at Jerusalem the feast of the dedication, and it was winter. And Jesus walked in the temple in Solomon's porch. Then came the Jews round about him, and said unto him, How long dost thou make us to doubt? If thou be the Christ, tell us plainly.

Jesus answered them, I told you, and ye believed not: the works that I do in my Father's name, they bear witness of me.

But ye believe not, because ye are not of my sheep, as I said unto you. My sheep hear my voice, and I know them, and they follow me: And I give unto them eternal life; and they shall never perish; neither shall any man pluck them out of my hand. My Father, which gave them me, is greater than all; and no man is able to pluck them out of my Father's hand. I and my Father are one."

We also learned from the Bible that when Yeshua (Jesus) came to earth, He was often referred to as the "Light of the World."

"In him [Yeshua (Jesus)] was life; and the life was the light of men. And the light shineth in darkness; and the darkness comprehended It not. (John 1: 4-5) KJV

Since my family members were Messianic believers, our main emphasis during Hanukkah was always on Yeshua (Jesus).

Because of the example Yeshua (Jesus) gave us, each of us is also called to be a light to the world. However, before we can share the light of Yeshua (Jesus), we must first become a light by accepting Yeshua (Jesus) as our Lord and Saviour.

"Let your light so shine before men, that they may see your good works, and glorify your Father which is in heaven."

(Matthew 5: 16) KJV

A Future Glory

In *(Isaiah 60: 1-3) KJV,* the prophet spoke about a future day when the light will bring restoration to Israel:

"Arise, shine; for thy light is come, and the glory of the Lord is risen upon thee. For, behold, the darkness shall cover the earth, and gross darkness the people: but the Lord shall arise upon thee, and his glory shall be seen upon thee.

And the Gentiles shall come to thy light, and kings to the brightness of thy rising."

Also, in *(Revelation 21: 22-27) KJV,* the Apostle John described a future time when the New Jerusalem, our glorious eternal dwelling place, will descend from Heaven. It will be lighted solely by the Glory of God and Yeshua (Jesus).

"And I saw no temple therein: for the Lord God Almighty and the Lamb [Yeshua (Jesus)] are the temple of it.

And the city had no need of the sun, neither of the moon, to shine in it: for the glory of God did lighten it and the Lamb is the light thereof.

And the nations of them which are saved shall walk in the light of it: and the kings of the earth do bring their glory and honour into it."

My View Today

When we accept Yeshua (Jesus) as our Messiah, He comes to live within us, rather than in a temple built by man. For that reason, our bodies are now called the "Temple of God." As I thought about this,

I also wondered how many people realize that. It made me want to be careful how I treated this temple. Then the thought came to me, "Are you desecrating your temple?" Anytime we violate our temple (body) with anything that is ungodly or sinful, we become like King Antiochus IV, who defiled the temple of God centuries ago. I decided to live for God, dedicating my temple (body) daily to the glory of God. May God's light of Hanukkah shine brightly in each of us. "Baruch HaShem,"

CHAPTER 8

THE CONCLUSION

"LIFT HIGH THE BANNER"

CHAPTER 8

THE CONCLUSION

Once this book is read and all the hidden mysteries and secrets are revealed, we can LIFT HIGH THE BANNER in a Godly victory procession, and everyone in my family can freely and openly praise El-Shaddai (All Mighty G-d). We invite descendants of other Messianic Sephardic families to join us in honoring Yeshua (Jesus), the King of Kings and Lord of Lords. For so long our ancestors have been hidden in remote areas, but now the day has come when their descendants no longer have to hide or cover up their heritage. When we see the BANNER FLYING, we will know that we have overcome the enemy, fear and anxiety, from our past, present and future. Stand with me now as the BANNER IS GOING BY, in tribute to our Creator, the Lord of the Universe. Together we will shout and sing praises to our God for His everlasting goodness and mercy.

Praise be to the LORD, the God of Israel, from everlasting to everlasting. Let all the people say, "Amen!"
Praise the LORD. (Psalm 106: 48) NIV

With great emotion, I give honor to His glorious name, for He alone is worthy of my praise!

Humbly, I submit:
Julie C. Marlow

GLOSSARY

Of Messianic Terms

GLOSSARY

This is a Glossary relating to the views of Messianic Jewish believers. All scripture references are from the King James Version of the Bible.

AARONIC BLESSING—Is the blessing that God commanded Aaron, the brother of Moses, to give to the children of Israel. *(Numbers 6: 22-27)*

ADONAI—The Hebrew name for God is translated as the **Lord Our God**, which was used instead of the name **Yahweh**, because it was considered so holy that devout Israelites would not pronounce it. To this day, when the **Shema** (the truth that followers of God testify to) is recited in Hebrew, the word **Adonai** replaces the holy name **Yahweh**.

ALIYAH—The word **aliyah,** Hebrew for **ascent** or **pilgrimage**, conveys the religious significance of the act of returning to Israel from the **Diaspora,** which referred to the time when the Jews were scattered all over the world. Throughout the centuries, generations of Jews have made **aliyah**, a means of fulfilling a religious obligation. *(Amos: 9: 14-15)*

ASCENSION—Forty days after the crucifixion and resurrection of Jesus, the risen Christ (celebrated at Easter), parted from His disciples and returned to the Father. The Bible records that it was a bodily disappearance by an upward movement into the sky. *(Mark 16: 19-20) (Luke 24: 50-51) (Acts 1: 9-11)*

ASHKENAZIM—From 1881 to 1914, Jews fled to the U.S. from **pogroms** (persecutions) in Russian ruled areas of Eastern Europe. German, Polish and Russian Jews are all called **Ashkenazim.**

BAPTISM—The ceremony or sacrament admitting a person into Christianity by immersing the individual in water as a symbol of washing away sin and of spiritual purification. It means a complete break with the past, a removal of sin and the start of a new life lived in the power given by Jesus Christ Himself. The baptism of Jesus is our example. For the believer, baptism is a testimony of faith and a pledge to walk in a newness of life in Jesus Christ. *(Matthew 3: 6-8; 3: 13-17) (Mark 1: 10-11) (Acts 2: 38-47) (Acts 10:44-48) (Romans 6: 3-5) (Mark 16:15-18)*

BCE—signifies *before Common Era*. This is synonymous with *BC* or *before Christ*.

BELIEVER—This term is sometimes used for Christian converts instead of the term *Christian*. By using the term *Believer*, the focus is on a person's commitment to following the Lord and a belief or trust in Christ that is necessary for salvation and essential to righteousness. *(Acts: 5: 12-14) (Romans 10: 9-10) (Galatians 3: 6-7) (1 Timothy 4: 12)*

CAPTIVITY—It usually refers to God's chosen people, the Israelites, being divinely punished by captivity or servitude. *(Leviticus 26: 33) (Deuteronomy 4: 27)*

CE—signifies *Common Era*. This is synonymous with *AD* or *Anno Domini* (in the year of our Lord), referring to the period after Christ was born.

CHRIST—The official title applied to *Jesus*, a Jew, and the Son of the Living God. He is the second person of the *Triune Godhead*: *God the Father*, *God the Son* and *God the Holy Spirit*. The Greek word **Christ** means the *Anointed One*. Some people incorrectly think Christ is a surname, as in **Jesus Christ**. Other accepted names for Him are *Messiah; Redeemer; Saviour; Lord; Rabbi; The Truth; The Way and The Life; Prince of Peace; The Word of God; God's Only Begotten Son; King of Kings; Lord of Lords; Good Shepherd; Lamb of God; The Perfect Sacrifice; Deliverer; Son of David; Rose of Sharon; Lilly of the Valleys; The Fulfillment of Prophecy; The Resurrection.* *(Matthew 16: 15-16) (Luke 2: 11) (John 1: 14) (Song of Solomon 2: 1) (Revelation 3: 20-22)*

CHRISTIAN—This term was first used for non-Jewish believers in Antioch, as recorded in the Book of Acts. In scripture, the term was never directly used for Jewish believers. The term *Messianic* was used.

This identified Jewish believers as followers of Jesus, the Messiah. *(Acts 11: 25-26)*

CHOSEN PEOPLE—The descendants of ***Abraham***, the Old Testament patriarch. His descendants are called the ***House of Israel***. This means that the Jewish people are the people of God. As ***God's chosen people,*** they are the object of His special concern and affection; they are called His ***first born***, His ***son*** and His ***beloved***. But, at the same time, they were given the responsibility and the obligation by covenants to obey Him in a unique way not required of other nations. *(Deuteronomy: 14: 2)*

CHURCH—An assembly of believers in Jesus Christ who gather together for the purpose of worship. The people comprising the early church were both Jewish and Gentile believers. The church had its beginning on the day of Pentecost at the coming of the Holy Spirit. It also includes all of the redeemed of the ages who belong to Christ. *(Acts 2: 44-47)*

CONGREGATION—Messianic congregations are gatherings of Jewish believers for the purpose of worshiping, teaching and praising Yeshua, Jesus as the Messiah. They are not called churches. They are called congregations (believers who gather for religious instruction). *(Psalms 111:1) (Hebrews 10: 23-25)*

CONVERSION—Biblically, conversion refers to repentance, i.e., turning to God. The term ***Converted Jew*** is not a term that is used by Messianic Jewish believers because they do not lose their Jewish descent. Messianic believers are those who have expressed their faith in Yeshua (Jesus) as their promised Messiah. (Acts 11: 26) (Acts 26: 28)

COVENANT—An agreement between two people, two groups of people, or, particularly, between God and His people, that promised His blessings in return for their obedience and devotion. The Old Covenant (Tenach or Old Testament) refers to the Old Covenant of the Law of Moses and the New Covenant (Brit Chadashah or New Testament) refers to the New Covenant of Grace. Through His sacrificial death, Jesus became the mediator of the New Covenant, bringing salvation and eternal life to all who trust in Him. The New Covenant is still in effect today and is freely offered to all mankind. *(Genesis 17: 7-8) (Hebrews 8: 7-10)*

CRYPTO-JEWS—Superficial Catholics in Spain, also known as **Marranos,** who practiced their Jewish faith in secret in order to escape persecution by the Spanish Inquisition.

DAY OF ATONEMENT—This Jewish holy day, named **Yom Kippur,** was first observed in the Old Testament. It was a day on which atonement for sins was made for all of Israel. It recognized man's inability to make atonement for himself. On this day, the Jewish High Priest first made atonement for himself and then for the sins of the people by sprinkling the blood of a sacrificial lamb on the altar, foreshadowing the one-for-all sacrifice of Jesus Christ. Then a second animal, called a scapegoat, representing the sins of the people, was released into the wilderness to symbolize pardon. (*Leviticus 23: 27-28) (Hebrews 10: 9-12))*

ERETZ-YISRAEL—This means the "Land Of Israel".

GOD—He is the **Creator** and the **Ruler** of the universe. He is the first person of the **Triune Godhead [Echad, meaning One or Unity]: God the Father**, **God the Son**, and **God the Holy Spirit**. The scriptures are full of declarations that there is only **One True God**. In the Old Testament, God revealed Himself to the Hebrews in various ways, including calling Himself **I Am** [meaning, I Am whatever you need]. In the New Testament, God revealed Himself in **Jesus Christ** as the **Only Begotten Son**. There are various Hebrew words which are translated as God: **Adoni, El Elohim, Jehovah** and **Yeshua**. Other ways of referring to God are: **Lord, Father, Almighty** and **Redeemer, etc.** *(Isaiah 40: 28) (Matthew 28: 18-20)*

HANUKKAH—It is called the **Feast of Dedication** *and the* **Feast of Lights**. It is an eight day celebration commemorating God's deliverance of the Israelites from their Maccabee oppressors. *(John 10: 22-23)*

HOLY SPIRIT—(Ruach HaKodesh)—The Holy Spirit is the third person of the **Triune Godhead**: (Echad) meaning unity or One, **God the Father, God the Son** and **God the Holy Spirit**. The power of the Holy Spirit was evidenced in the miraculous birth of Yeshua (Jesus). *(Matthew 1:18-25)*. The Holy Spirit descended upon Yeshua (Jesus) at his baptism in the River Jordan. *(Luke 3: 21-22)* Jesus promised His disciples that after His departure, He would send them another **Comforter,** who would abide in them forever. He would be their **Helper, Teacher** and **Advocate.** He would endue them with the power to boldly proclaim the gospel message. He was first given to the disciples in the Upper Room on the Day of Pentecost, after the Passover *(Acts 1: 5-8)* and the resurrection of Jesus *(John 14: 16-17) (Romans 8: 8-11)*

LADINO—A 15ᵀᴴ century Judeo-Spanish language that was spoken by Sephardic (Sefarad in Hebrew) Jews who were expelled from Spain and Portugal from 1492 through the 1500's. They brought the Ladino language with them to North America, and, eventually, to the Territories of New Mexico and Colorado.

MARRANOS—This was the name given by Catholics in Spain and Portugal to Jews who had converted to Catholicism for fear of religious persecution, but who secretly continued to practice Jewish traditions. The word **Marranos** means "**swine**," replaced for the most part by the word **Crypto-Jews**.

MESSIAH—This term is used instead of **Christ**. Messiah is derived from the Hebrew word **Mashiach**, meaning **Anointed One**. Christ is derived from the Greek word **Christos**, meaning **Anointed One**

MESSIANIC JEWISH BELIEVERS—These are Jews who believe that **Yeshua (Jesus)** is the **Messiah**, the **Anointed One,** who was the fulfillment of Old Testament prophecies. The first Jewish believers joined together to form the early church of the first century. They were persecuted because of their belief in Jesus. Later on, their descendants were scattered throughout the world, and, surprisingly, even to North America and remote areas in Colorado and New Mexico. The Jewish people as a whole have experienced several times of scattering throughout their history.

MIKVEH—A ritual, of immersion, or baptism, in water, which is usually performed only once in a lifetime. When one is baptized, it is for separation from the world. We are called to live a life that is holy unto God. Therefore, once baptized as adults, we try to live that separated holy life, in accordance with God's instructions in both the Old and New Covenants. The baptism of Jesus is our example. *(Matthew 3: 13-17) (Matthew 28: 18-20)*

PASSOVER—It is a Jewish holy day commemorating God's miraculous deliverance of the Israelites from slavery in Egypt, as recorded in the **Book of Exodus**. The Hebrew word is **Pesach**. Passover prophetically refers to God's plan for the redemption of mankind in a dramatic and miraculous way.

ROSH HASHANAH—The words mean the **Head of the Year** or the **Jewish New Year**. It is a holy day for the Jewish people to take stock of their spiritual condition and make necessary changes to ensure that the upcoming year will be pleasing to God. The day begins with the blowing of the **shofar** (ram's horn), which the Apostle Paul prophetically related to a future gathering up of believers to meet Jesus in the air, commonly called the **Rapture**. *(1 Thessalonians 4: 16-18)*

RUACH HAKODESH—This term is the Hebrew name for the **Holy Spirit**.

SEPHARDIC—This is a name given to Jews who migrated to other parts of the world from Spain and Portugal because of religious persecution by the Spanish Inquisition. These Jews became known as Sephardic Jews, after **Sephardim**, the Hebrew name for Spain. The Sephardic Jews spread out all over the Mediterranean lands, including Greece and Turkey. Some settled in Western Europe, particularly Great Britain, the Netherlands and France, and some later migrated overseas, most notably to the Americas.

SHABBAT—It is the Jewish day of worship and rest, established when God rested after the six days of creation. The fourth of the Ten Commandments called for the Sabbath to be observed and kept holy. The word **Shabbat** means **to rest**. It is a time when all work ceases. The Old Testament Sabbath fell on the seventh day of the week, or the Jewish Saturday. *(Genesis 2: 1-3) (Exodus 20: 8-11)*

SONSHIP OF BELIEVERS—*"For as many as are led by the Spirit of God, they are the **Sons of God**." (Romans 8: 14)*

SPANISH INQUISITION—King Ferdinand and Queen Isabella of Spain instituted an **Inquisition**, or a court of inquiry, to enforce strict religious standards for all Catholics. It was considered the darkest period in Spain's history.

SUKKOT—It refers to the season of bringing in the latter harvest. It is the Jewish *Thanksgiving*, celebrating the fact that God has provided for us and has made His habitation with us. *(Leviticus 23: 39-43)*

YESHUA—*Yeshua* is the Hebrew name for *Jesus*, the Messiah, which has the root meaning of "*salvation.*" Jesus is often referred to as *Yeshua HaMashiach*, meaning *Jesus the Messiah, and The Anointed One.*

YOM KIPPUR—*Yom Kippur*, or *Day of Atonement*, has long been considered the most holy day on the Jewish biblical calendar. It occurs ten days after *Rosh Hashanah*, the *Jewish New Year*. It illustrates regeneration for those who accept and follow God's way of atonement and forgiveness of sin by way of Jesus' sacrifice on the cross for the sins of mankind. There is no more important theme in the Holy Scriptures than receiving atonement for sins in God's prescribed manner.

Notice:

I do not claim to know many of the Hebrew terms personally, since I did not hear or learn Hebrew in my childhood. Our congregation was made up solely of (Secret) Sephardic Messianic believers like me who learned only from the Holy Bible and from the oral history given by family members. It was not until I was an adult and had left my hometown that I was in contact with non-Messianic Jewish people.

It was for obvious reasons that we had to be very secretive about our beliefs, but my heart always yearned to be in a Messianic Congregation where I could hear and learn more about our faith. Today, I enjoy going to Messianic Jewish Conferences, where I delight in the teaching, music, and dance. It is such a blessing!

For more detailed information about the Hebrew meaning of words, please check the <u>Complete Jewish Bible,</u> translation by Stern, David H. (Jewish New Testament Publications, Inc. Clarksville, Maryland USA. c. 1998

SOURCES
FOR THE BOOK

(BIBLE SOURCES)
And
(GENERAL SOURCES)

BIBLE SOURCES
FOR THIS BOOK

Holy Bible: King James Version Containing the Old and New Testament. (Iowa Falls: World Bible Publishers, 1979)

Life Application Bible: New International Version. (Wheaton, Illinois: Tyndale House Publishers, Inc., 1991)

The Holy Bible: Old and New Testaments in the King James Version. Translated out of the Original Tongues and with Previous Translations Diligently Compared and Revised. (Nashville: Thomas Nelson Publishers, 1976)

The Living Bible: Paraphrased. (Wheaton, Illinois: Tyndale House Publishers, 1971)

The Thompson Chain-Reference Bible: Fourth Improved Edition. King James Version. Ed. Frank Charles Thompson. (Indianapolis: B. B. Kirkbride Bible Co., Inc., 1964)

SOURCES FOR THIS BOOK

(GENERAL)

Abraham, Abram Kenneth, Compiled by. Promises of the Messiah. (Uhrichsville, OH: Barbour and Company, Inc., 1987)

Anderson, Ken. Where to Find It in the Bible: The Ultimate A to Z Resource. (Nashville: Thomas Nelson Publishers, 1996)

Ausubel, Nathan. The Book of Jewish Knowledge. (New York: Crown Publishers, Inc, 1964)

Bernis, Jonathan. What Happened to the Lost Tribes of Israel? The Scattering of the Tribes of Israel. March/April 2005.

Birmingham, Stephen. The Grandees: America's Sephardic Elite. (New York: Syracuse University Press, 1971)

Christofferson, Nancy. La Veta the First 40 Years: A History of La Veta, Colorado. (Privately printed, 2001)

Dimont, Max I. Jews, God and History. (New York: The New American Library, Inc., 1962.

Erdmann's, Family Encyclopedia of the Bible. Ed. Pat Alexander. (England: Lion Publishing, 1978)

Encyclopedia of Zionism and Israel. Ed. Raphael Patai. (New York: Herzl Press/ McGraw-Hill, 1971)

Encyclopedia Judaica. (Jerusalem: Keter Publishing House, 1972) "Family, or Last, Names." The World Book Encyclopedia. (Chicago: Field Enterprises Educational Corporation, 1976)

Finkelstein, Norman H. The Other 1492 Jewish Settlement in the New World. (New York: Charles Scribner's Sons, 1989)

Gehman, Henry Snyder, Editor. The New Westminster Dictionary of the Bible. (Philadelphia: Westminster Press, 1970)

Gerber, Jane S. The Jews of Spain: A History of the Sephardic Experience. (New York: The Free Press, 1992)

Gilbert, Martin. The Atlas of Jewish History: Third Ed. (New York: Dorset Press, 1976) Maps: #46, #47, and #49 and #56.

Harris, Reader. The Lost Tribes of Israel. (London: Robert Banks & Son, 1907)

"Indian, American," The World Book Encyclopedia: Volume 10, (I), p 138 A-CS 1976.I, Ed. Garbarino, Merwyn S. "Indians of the Southwest." (Chicago: Field Enterprises Educational Corporation, 1976)

Jacobs, Janet Liebman. Hidden Heritage: The Legacy of the Crypto-Jews. (Berkeley: University of California Press, 2002)

Justin, Daniel. Jewish Roots, Pacific Palisades: (Dover, 1986)

Kasdan, Barney. God's Appointed Times. (Baltimore: Lederer Messianic Publications, 1993)

Lecompte, Janet. Pueblo, Hardscrabble, Greenhorn: Society on the High Plains, 1832-1856. (Norman: University of Oklahoma Press, 1978)

Martin, Bernice. (Edited and Annotated). Frontier Eyewitness. Diary of John Lawrence, 1867-1908. (Monte Vista, Colorado: San Luis Valley Historian, n.d.)

Netanyahu, B. The Marranos of Spain: From the Late 14th to the Early 16th Century, According to Contemporary Hebrew Sources. (Ithaca, New York: Cornell University Press, 1996)

Rosen, Moishe and Ceil Rosen. Christ in the Passover. (Chicago: Mood Press 1978)

Sanchez, Dell F. The Last Exodus. (Niles, Illinois: Mall Publishing Company 1998)

Sanchez, Dell F. The Marrano Jews, (Jewish Voice Today) March/April 2005. P.6.

Strong, James. The New Strong's Exhaustive Concordance of the Bible. (Nashville: Thomas Nelson Publishers, 1990)

The Saguache County Museum. Images of the Past: Places and People, Volume 1. (Saguache, Colorado: The Saguache County Museum, 1996)

Tobias, Henry J. A History of the Jews in New Mexico. (Albuquerque: University of New Mexico Press, 1990)

The Book of A Thousand Tongues. Ed. Eric M. North. (London: United Bible Societies, 1939 p 1206)

Tushar, Olibama Lopez. The People of El Valle. A History of the Spanish Colonials in the San Luis Valley. (Pueblo, Colorado: El Escritorio, 1992

"Welcome! To The Scenic Highway of Legends." (2003). Visitor's Guide 2nd Edition 2003, Number 5.

Encyclopedia http://enc.wikipedia.org/wiki/File: COA_cordoba, spain.svg.

Wong, Amy Ng. God from A to Z. (Uhrichsville, Ohio: Barbour Publishing, Inc., 2001)

Zimmerman, Martha. Celebrate the Feasts. (Minneapolis: Bethany House Publishers, 1981)

THE AUTHOR'S BIOGRAPHY
AND PHOTOGRAPH

Julie C. Marlow

AUTHOR'S BIOGRAPHY

This is Julie's Marlow's first book, originally intended to be shared only with her family, but when she found secrets that had been hid for generations she decided she had to share it with others. She made it her God inspired mission to confirm what her parents and maternal grandparents had told her about their Jewish heritage and their fear of religious persecution.

She has a Bachelor of Science Degree in Education and a Master of Science Degree in Library Science. She was Assistant Professor of Library Science, Reference Librarian and Bibliographic Instructor at Gainesville State College, Gainesville. She retired in 1998.

She's been a teacher, high school media specialist, children's librarian and Sunday school teacher. She resides with her husband Arthur, in Gainesville, Georgia, has two grown children and four grandchildren.

Julie C. Marlow
P.O. Box 90
Oakwood, GA 30566

CPSIA information can be obtained at www.ICGtesting.com
Printed in the USA
LVOW06s0929220913

353428LV00002B/4/P